Lecture Notes of the Institute for Computer Sciences, Social Informatics and Telecommunications Engineering 502

The LNICST series publishes ICST's conferences, symposia and workshops.
LNICST reports state-of-the-art results in areas related to the scope of the Institute.
The type of material published includes

- Proceedings (published in time for the respective event)
- Other edited monographs (such as project reports or invited volumes)

LNICST topics span the following areas:

- General Computer Science
- E-Economy
- E-Medicine
- Knowledge Management
- Multimedia
- Operations, Management and Policy
- Social Informatics
- Systems

João L. Afonso · Vitor Monteiro ·
José Gabriel Pinto
Editors

Sustainable Energy for Smart Cities

4th EAI International Conference, SESC 2022
Braga, Portugal, November 16–18, 2022
Proceedings

Springer

Editors
João L. Afonso ⓘ
University of Minho
Guimaraes, Portugal

Vitor Monteiro ⓘ
University of Minho
Guimaraes, Portugal

José Gabriel Pinto ⓘ
University of Minho
Guimaraes, Portugal

ISSN 1867-8211   ISSN 1867-822X (electronic)
Lecture Notes of the Institute for Computer Sciences, Social Informatics
and Telecommunications Engineering
ISBN 978-3-031-33978-3   ISBN 978-3-031-33979-0 (eBook)
https://doi.org/10.1007/978-3-031-33979-0

This Springer imprint is published by the registered company Springer Nature Switzerland AG
The registered company address is: Gewerbestrasse 11, 6330 Cham, Switzerland

Preface

We are delighted to launch the proceedings of the fourth edition of the International Conference on Sustainable Energy for Smart Cities (SESC), which was sponsored by the European Alliance for Innovation (EAI) and with close collaboration and organization by the University of Minho, Portugal. As with the previous editions of SESC, also this edition was organized in alignment with the Smart City 360° Summit Event and it was a fully-fledged online conference, due to the pandemic situation around the world. The principal goal of the SESC 2022 conference was to present a multidisciplinary scientific online conference encompassing the emergent and complex technical facets of smart cities. Enclosed within the scope of smart cities, subjects relating to sustainable energy were also debated at SESC 2022 as a vital paradigm to guarantee an equilibrium between economic growth and environmental sustainability, ensuring a contribution to decreasing the consequences of climate change.

The SESC 2022 technical program includes ten full papers in the main conference tracks covering topics aligned with smart cities and sustainable energy, which were allocated among four sessions. A double-blinded peer review process was used for each submitted paper and a minimum of three reviews was ensured for each paper, where the reviewers were selected according to the topics covered in the papers. Concerning the committees, the cooperation with the EAI team was significant for the success of the SESC 2022 conference. In addition, we would like to exhibit our gratitude to all the members of the Technical Program Committee, which were vital to a high-quality technical program and to guarantee the high-quality process of peer review. Last, but not least, we would like to thank all the reviewers, with origin from different countries around the world, who were particularly invited based on the distinct areas of expertise included in the SESC 2022 conference.

The SESC 2022 conference was a recognized scientific meeting for all academics, researchers, and practitioners, presenting the occasion to debate technical, scientific, and technological guidelines focusing on smart cities. Associated with the success of the SESC 2022 conference, manifested in the diverse subjects covered in the papers given in this volume, we are expecting a successful and stimulating future series of SESC conferences.

João L. Afonso
Vitor Monteiro
José Gabriel Pinto

Organization

Steering Committee

Imrich Chlamtac	University of Trento, Italy
Joao L. Afonso	University of Minho, Portugal
Vitor Monteiro	University of Minho, Portugal
Gabriel Pinto	University of Minho, Portugal

Organizing Committee

General Chairs

Joao L. Afonso	University of Minho, Portugal
Vitor Monteiro	University of Minho, Portugal
Gabriel Pinto	University of Minho, Portugal

Technical Program Committee Chairs

Joao L. Afonso	University of Minho, Portugal
Vitor Monteiro	University of Minho, Portugal
Gabriel Pinto	University of Minho, Portugal

Technical Program Committee Co-chair

Carlos Couto	University of Minho, Portugal

Web Chair

Jose Afonso	University of Minho, Portugal

Publicity and Social Media Chairs

Sergio Coelho	University of Minho, Portugal
Amira Haddouk	University of Tunis, Tunisia

Workshops Chair

Luiz Cardoso   University of Minho, Portugal

Sponsorship and Exhibits Chair

Paula Ferreira   University of Minho, Portugal

Publications Chair

Luis Barros   University of Minho, Portugal

Panels Chair

Carlos Martins   University of Minho, Portugal

Tutorials Chair

Helena Fernández   University of Minho, Portugal

Demos Chair

Jose Cunha   University of Minho, Portugal

Posters and PhD Track Chair

Joao Sepulveda   University of Minho, Portugal

Local Chair

Julio Martins   University of Minho, Portugal

Students' Participation Chair

Nuno Rodrigues   University of Minho, Portugal

Technical Program Committee

Carlos Couto	University of Minho, Portugal
Edson H. Watanabe	Federal University of Rio de Janeiro, Brazil
João A. Peças Lopes	University of Porto, Portugal
Walter Issamu Suemitsu	Federal University of Rio de Janeiro, Brazil

Maurício Aredes	Federal University of Rio de Janeiro, Brazil
Guilherme Rolim	Federal University of Rio de Janeiro, Brazil
Carlos Hengeler Antunes	University of Coimbra, Portugal
Adriano Carvalho	University of Porto, Portugal
João P. S. Catalão	University of Porto, Portugal
Antonio Lima	State University of Rio de Janeiro, Brazil
António Pina Martins	University of Porto, Portugal
Hfaiedh Mechergui	University of Tunis, Tunisia
Rosaldo Rossetti	University of Porto, Portugal
Luis Monteiro	State University of Rio de Janeiro, Brazil
João P. P. Carmo	University of São Paulo, Brazil
A. Caetano Monteiro	University of Minho, Portugal
Marcello Mezaroba	UDESC – Santa Catarina State University, Brazil
Luis Martins	University of Minho, Portugal
Orlando Soares	Instituto Politécnico de Bragança, Portugal
Paulo Pereirinha	University of Coimbra, Portugal
Marcelo Cavalcanti	Federal University of Pernambuco, Brazil
Jose A. Afonso	University of Minho, Portugal
José L. Lima	Instituto Politécnico de Bragança, Portugal
Carlos Felgueiras	Polytechnic of Porto (ISEP), Portugal
Amira Haddouk	University of Tunis, Tunisia
Joao C. Ferreira	ISCTE – University Institute of Lisbon, Portugal
Stefani Freitas	Federal University of Tocantins, Brazil
Julio S. Martins	University of Minho, Portugal
Kleber Oliveira	Federal University of Paraíba, Brazil
Joao L. Monteiro	University of Minho, Portugal
Mohamed Tanta	Vestas Wind Systems A/S, Portugal
M. J. Sepúlveda	University of Minho, Portugal
Gerardo J. Osório	Portucalense University, Portugal
Vladimir Sousa Santos	Universidad de la Costa, Colombia
Mattia Ricco	University of Bologna, Italy
Jelena Loncarski	University of Bologna, Italy
Riccardo Mandrioli	University of Bologna, Italy
Hani Vahedi	DCBEL Company, Canada
Mario Porru	University of Cagliari, Italy
Vincenzo Cirimele	University of Bologna, Italy
Sheldon Williamson	Ontario Tech University, Canada
Cassiano Rech	Federal University of Santa Maria (UFSM), Brazil
Nguyen Van Nghia	University of Transport and Communications, Vietnam
Dang Quoc Vuong	Hanoi University of Science and Technology, Vietnam

Contents

Electric Mobility; Power Electronics; Renewable Energy

Energy; Demand Response; Technical-Economic Analysis

Forecasting of Day-Ahead Wind Speed/electric Power by Using a Hybrid Machine Learning Algorithm

Atilla Altıntaş[1]([✉]), Lars Davidson[1][ID], and Ola Carlson[2][ID]

[1] Division of Fluid Dynamics, Department of Mechanics and Maritime Sciences, Chalmers University of Technology, 41296 Gothenburg, Sweden
altintas@chalmers.se
[2] Department of Electrical Engineering, Chalmers University of Technology, 41296 Gothenburg, Sweden

Abstract. The amount of energy that has to be delivered for the following day is currently predicted by power system operators using day-ahead load forecasts. With the use of this forecast, generation resources can be committed a day in advance, some of them may require several hours' notice to be ready to produce power the following day. In order to determine how much wind power will be available for each hour of the following day, power systems with large penetrations of wind generation rely on day-ahead predictions. The main objective of this study is to improve the day-ahead forecasting of wind power by improving the forecasting method using machine learning. A hybrid approach, which combines a mode decomposition method, Empirical Mode Decomposition (EMD), with Support Vector Regression (SVR), is used. The results suggest that using Support Vector Regression together with the hybrid method, which includes the Empirical Mode Decomposition to predictions can improve the accuracy of predictions. Higher accuracy forecasting of wind power is expected to improve the planning of dispatchable energy generation and pricing for the day-ahead power market.

Keywords: Wind energy · wind turbine · Empirical Mode Decomposition (EMD) · forecasting · machine learning · renewable energy · grid integration · energy market

1 Introduction

Among available renewable energy sources, wind energy has the largest potential [5,17]. Wind turbines are connected to the medium voltage distribution grid or the regional transmission grid. In order to transport the energy with low losses, the electric grid is usually designed as a high voltage transmission grid that is

---

This work is supported by the Chalmers University, Energy Area of Advance.

J. L. Afonso et al. (Eds.): SESC 2022, LNICST 502, pp. 3–11, 2023.
https://doi.org/10.1007/978-3-031-33979-0_1

connected to centralized production units. Since high voltages are impractical and dangerous to use, voltage is transformed to lower levels and distributed to the end users via a distribution grid. The main challenge when operating the power system is to keep the system in balance, i.e. to keep the balance in supply and demand. Integration of the wind power into the electric grid is problematic since the varying nature of the wind speed gives fluctuations in the produced wind power [17].

Sweden has the clear goal of 100% renewable electricity production by 2040. The Swedish Energy Agency's assessment shows that wind turbines will produce 60–90 TWh. Many new wind turbines need to be built to achieve that goal and the total supply needs for electric power production is estimated to be about 180 TWh. Although, recent studies show a much larger need of electric power in the future. Currently, 61% of Swedish electricity generation comes from hydro- and wind power. The Swedish Energy Agency estimates that in order to achieve this goal, the nation will need to install an extra 2.5 to 6 TWh of renewable energy capacity per year between 2030 and 2040 [7,10]. The growth of wind power that is connected to the electric grid requires wind farms appear more like conventional power plants and hence it will be necessary to forecast the produced power.

Recently, efforts to improve forecasting methodologies have also included the use of EMD in many areas from wind energy to financial time series ([3,6,9,11,13,15]). EMD is a method which decomposes a complex time series of data into its frequency components i.e so called intrinsinc mode functions (IMFs) ([3,8,9]). EMD divides data into its IMFs, which represent a number of high to low frequency components. The high frequency component corresponds to short-term changes, and low frequency component corresponds to long-term changes. By using different combination of the frequency components of the data we can predict both short and long-term predictions much more accurately compared to using the entire data set. The general idea behind the use of EMD for forecasting purposes is to separate the data into its components which reduces the complexity, separates the trends of different time scales. In this way the accuracy of the forecasting is improved.

In order to determine how much wind power will be available for each hour of the following day, power systems with large penetrations of wind generation rely on day-ahead wind predictions (Piwko and Jordan [12] and Rintamäki et al. [16]). In this study we improve the accuracy of the day-ahead wind speed forecasting by using a hybrid EMD-SVR method. The measured power is used as input data and selected IMFs of the power are used as influence parameters for the SVR regression model.

2   Theory and Method

2.1   Scale Decomposition by Empirical Mode Decomposition

EMD is predicated on the idea that any data signal is made up of a number of basic intrinsic oscillations, with the raw signal being a superposition of these oscillations (refer to Ref. [3] for further analysis). Each mode is referred to as an IMF that satisfies the two conditions; the local extrema and zero-crossing numbers must be equal or differ by one at the most and the mean of the curve that is constructed by connecting the maxima and minima should be zero [8].

2.2   SVR Method

The Support Vector Regression (SVR) is an algorithm for machine learning, which is a variant of Support Vector Machine (SVM) (Qiu et al. [14], Altıntaş et al. [4]). Consider a time-series data,

$$D = (X_i, y_i), 1 \le i \le N,$$

where X_i represents the ith element and y_i corresponds the target output data. The SVR function, f, is a linear function that relates the input and output data as $f(X_i) = \omega^T \phi(X_i) + b$, where ω, b, and $\phi(X_i)$ are the weight vector, bias, and the function that maps the input vector X into a higher dimensional feature space, respectively.

Python programming language and scikit-learn 1.1.2 package has been used for SVR. The radial basis function (RBF) is chosen as the kernel function, then Kernel function written as:

$$K(X_i, X_j) = exp(-\gamma X_i - X_j{}^2), \tag{1}$$

where the parameter γ, defines the degree to which the effect of a single example of training reaches. In this study parameters are set to, $\gamma = 0.96$, $C = 1.0$, which balances the trade-off between the complexity of the model and its generalization ability, and the maximum error, ϵ, is set to 0.03, and are used for all the predictions.

2.3   Wind Power Data

The data are from the Röbergsfjället wind farm which is situated at Röbergskullen in the southernmost section of the Swedish municipality of Vansbro (60160 49.8"N, 14120 59.6"E) (see Fig. 1). The wind farm was constructed in 2007, with its highest point being at 543 m above sea level. There are 284 m between the wind farm's highest and lowest elevations. It consists of eight Vestas V90-2MW horizontal axis wind turbines [2]. The wind turbine that has been used for this study is highlighted with the red pin in Fig. 1(a) and also the area is highlighted in a larger map in Fig. 1(b).

The data consist of a list of records including power, hub direction, pitch angle, rotor RPM, temperature, wind direction and wind speed for the period of 21 June 2017 to 3 February 2019. The data are recorded every second.

Wind turbines measure the wind speed with an anemometer which is installed at a specific location on the nacelle. This anemometer is installed behind the blades thus exposed to created turbulence by the rotor blades. Therefore we

(a) Röbergsfjället wind farm. The data is from the wind turbine pointed with the red pin.

(b) Location of the windfarm Röbergsfjället.

Fig. 1. Wind farm and turbine location [1].

can not trust the wind speed measured in the downstream wake area, and wind direction is also not trusted for the same reason. Moreover, it is a pointwise measurement, however, the wind speed field that creates power is the rotor plane area which is far from homogeneous. For these reasons we can not use wind speed from the anemometer. In this study, output power history data has been used.

The three months of data has been used from 21 June 2017 to 20 August 2017. Thus a seasonal wind behaviour has been tried to be captured. For the same reason, the data between 11:00 to 17:00 has been used. The power data of the turbine are averaged over 10 min of time windows. For instance, the window 11:00–11:10 represents the data that has been averaged over 10 min in the given interval. There are missing records, meaning that in the given second the turbine has generated no power, which is excluded.

The predictions are made for every 10 min averaged time-window between 11:00–17:00, therefore thirty-five time-windows are used for forecasting. The data have been split into a training and a test part. The last day of the data which is 20 August 2017 is the test part, i.e the part to predict using the training data. The previous days' 10 min time-window has been used as the feature to forecast the next day's 10 min time-window, i.e., time-window 11:00–11:10 for the training days enters the process to forecast the test day's time-window, 11:10–11:20. The part of the data (for 11:00 to 12:00 for 92 days) which is split into ten minutes time windows are given in Fig. 2(a)).

In the EMD-SVR hybrid method, EMD used as a preprocessor to SVR. EMD splits data into IMFs and each IMF is a feature (input) for SVR. IMFs are frequency modes that are obtained by applying EMD to the original data

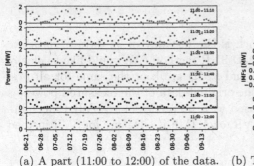 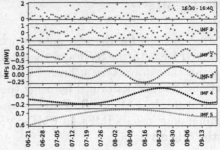

(a) A part (11:00 to 12:00) of the data.   (b) The upper signal is the raw data, and the subsequent five signals are the IMFs obtained by applying EMD to the raw data.

Fig. 2. Raw data and IMFs.

(raw data). The sum of all IMFs is equal to the original data. In Fig. 2(b), the original data of average power 11:00–11:10 and its IMFs' obtained by EMD are given. The data set has been split into its IMFs by limiting the number of IMFs to five, the fifth IMF is including the residual. Each five IMF have been an input for SVR. The data are scaled by Min-Max scaling method to an interval of $[0, 1]$ before the SVR process. The combinations of the outputs are the predictions. That process is repeated for all thirty-five time-window predictions in the EMD-SVR hybrid method. A process of EMD combined with SVR is given in Fig. 3.

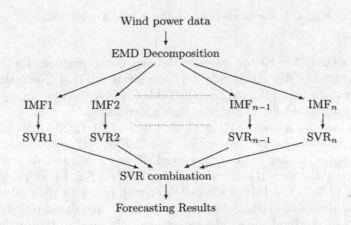

Fig. 3. Process schema of EMD-SVR method.

3   Results

The predictions for the test data which is the last day of 92 days of data are obtained for both the SVR and the EMD-SVR method. We would like to clarify that all the parameters in both SVR and EMD are kept the same for all predictions. SVR is performed by using the original data of the measured power as the feature. In EMD-SVR, EMD is used as a preprocessor to SVR that splits original data into its IMFs. In EMD-SVR, each IMF is a feature for SVR instead of the original data.

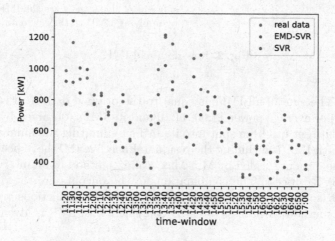

Fig. 4. Power predictions for the day 20 August 2022.

A total of thirty-five 10-min averaged time-window predictions for the hours, 11:00–17:00, for the day 20 August 2017 are given in Fig. 4. Normalized root mean square error (nRMSE) are given in Table 1, where the best approximation is given in a separate column and also highlighted in red.

Only for the time windows, 11:30–11:40, 12:10–12:20, 12:20–12:30 and 13:50–14:00, does raw data predict better than the IMF or IMF combinations. That means that approximately 90% of the cases IMF and combinations provide better prediction than using the raw data as feature (see Fig. 4 and Table 1). The combination of IMF 1 + IMF 2 agrees better with real data than all the other IMF combinations and original data for the total of nine cases, that is approximately 25% of the total cases. The lowest error obtained in the predictions is 0.4% and the maximum error is 18%.

Table 1. The power prediction errors for the time between 11:00–17:00, for the day 20 August 2017, for 10 min averaged time-windows (see Fig. 4). nRMSE = normalized root mean square error.

	Original data	nRMSE												Best Approximation
		IMF 1	IMF 2	IMF 3	IMF 4	Residual	Total IMFs	IMFs 1+2	IMFs 2+3	IMFs 3+4	IMFs 1+2+3	IMFs 1+2+3+4	IMFs 4+Residual	
11:10-11:20	0.214	0.372	0.692	0.682	0.734	0.712	0.797	0.066	0.376	0.418	0.246	0.512	0.449	IMFs 1+2
11:20-11:30	0.215	0.561	0.670	0.615	1.02	0.634	0.480	0.234	0.289	0.644	0.145	0.118	0.663	IMFs 1+2+3+4
11:30-11:40	0.074	0.093	0.616	0.604	0.675	0.749	1.250	0.286	0.222	0.280	0.681	1.0	0.423	Original data
11:40-11:50	0.242	0.439	0.724	0.776	0.798	0.516	0.738	0.163	0.502	0.574	0.056	0.257	0.317	IMFs 1+2+3
11:50-12:00	0.070	0.367	0.693	0.643	0.914	0.601	0.773	0.063	0.337	0.557	0.290	0.374	0.515	IMFs 1+2
12:00-12:10	0.193	0.224	0.790	0.582	0.674	0.702	1.01	0.017	0.375	0.259	0.397	0.722	0.380	IMFs 1+2
12:10-12:20	0.023	0.150	0.608	0.504	0.445	0.359	1.86	0.176	0.174	0.044	0.668	1.22	0.192	Original data
12:20-12:30	0.005	0.385	0.782	0.433	0.630	0.570	1.18	0.170	0.218	0.062	0.391	0.761	0.203	Original data
12:30-12:40	0.369	0.843	0.888	0.512	0.697	0.562	0.489	0.731	0.401	0.209	0.243	0.045	0.262	IMFs 1+2+3+4
12:40-12:50	0.165	0.345	0.447	0.494	1.18	0.019	1.50	0.202	0.053	0.676	0.706	0.524	0.202	Residual
12:50-13:00	0.152	0.372	0.309	0.004	0.855	0.372	2.09	0.313	0.694	0.148	1.31	1.46	0.224	IMF 3
13:00-13:10	0.067	0.523	0.505	0.397	0.672	0.361	1.53	0.031	0.090	0.072	0.569	0.894	0.032	IMFs 1+2
13:10-13:20	0.475	0.401	0.734	0.587	0.491	0.300	1.48	0.136	0.322	0.079	0.273	0.780	0.207	IMFs 3+4
13:20-13:30	0.343	0.973	0.719	0.751	0.709	0.547	0.291	0.694	0.473	0.464	0.448	0.158	0.259	IMFs 1+2+3+4
13:30-13:40	0.149	0.639	0.566	0.779	0.803	0.612	0.592	0.207	0.347	0.583	0.009	0.206	0.417	IMFs 1+2+3
13:40-13:50	0.334	0.293	0.913	0.731	0.671	0.931	0.453	0.207	0.644	0.403	0.056	0.384	0.603	IMFs 1+2+3
13:50-14:00	0.008	0.018	0.879	0.542	0.497	0.622	1.43	0.098	0.422	0.040	0.556	1.05	0.120	Original data
14:00-14:10	0.168	0.084	0.602	0.933	0.815	0.605	1.12	0.479	0.538	0.751	0.546	0.728	0.423	IMF 1
14:10-14:20	0.515	0.630	0.925	0.899	0.873	0.774	0.108	0.557	0.826	0.774	0.459	0.334	0.647	Total IMFs
14:20-14:30	0.249	0.182	0.624	0.576	0.839	0.585	1.18	0.187	0.203	0.418	0.610	0.768	0.427	IMF 1
14:30-14:40	0.132	0.556	0.553	0.602	0.574	0.751	0.956	0.109	0.158	0.179	0.283	0.709	0.325	IMFs 1+2
14:40-14:50	0.147	0.477	0.504	0.629	0.480	0.557	1.34	0.013	0.135	0.110	0.382	0.901	0.036	IMFs 1+2
14:50-15:00	0.098	0.308	0.377	0.915	0.595	0.580	1.21	0.311	0.293	0.511	0.395	0.796	0.179	IMFs 4+residual
15:00-15:10	0.172	0.436	0.653	0.624	0.863	0.594	0.818	0.091	0.278	0.488	0.281	0.416	0.458	IMFs 1+2
15:10-15:20	0.151	0.236	0.695	0.451	0.573	0.277	2.22	0.540	0.151	0.025	1.083	1.509	0.140	IMFs 3+4
15:20-15:30	0.046	0.167	0.167	0.052	0.133	0.069	4.14	0.994	0.763	1.07	1.93	3.07	1.20	IMF 3
15:30-15:40	0.404	0.566	0.368	0.072	0.577	0.108	2.52	0.061	0.552	0.342	0.985	1.40	0.537	IMFs 1+2
15:40-15:50	0.109	0.195	0.452	0.577	0.265	0.323	2.17	0.347	0.031	0.152	0.768	1.50	0.405	IMFs 2+3
15:50-16:00	0.215	0.365	0.548	0.511	0.537	0.230	1.79	0.080	0.062	0.051	0.566	1.02	0.226	IMFs 3+4
16:00-16:10	0.349	0.400	0.332	0.273	0.711	0.244	2.51	0.261	0.383	0.008	0.981	1.26	0.530	IMFs 3+4
16:10-16:20	0.223	0.273	0.152	0.340	0.577	0.479	2.16	0.568	0.501	0.080	1.22	1.64	0.058	IMFs 4+residual
16:20-16:30	0.443	0.540	0.781	0.417	0.528	0.640	1.08	0.323	0.199	0.049	0.258	0.725	0.170	IMFs 3+4
16:30-16:40	0.083	0.181	0.359	0.254	0.199	0.083	3.27	0.820	0.377	0.537	1.56	2.36	0.711	Residual
16:40-16:50	0.380	0.327	0.426	0.007	0.533	0.152	2.85	0.239	0.559	0.453	1.23	1.69	0.616	IMF 3
16:50-17:00	0.220	0.714	0.444	0.336	0.539	0.602	3.23	0.157	0.888	0.793	1.17	1.63	1.05	IMFs 1+2

4   Conclusion

In this study, an EMD-based decoupling procedure is applied as a preprocessor to SVR to improve the day-ahead wind power forecasting. First, IMFs are obtained by applying EMD to the original data, each IMF is used as a feature for SVR instead of the original data. The prediction results are compared for combinations of the IMFs and the original data. The data set has been split into 10 min time windows and a previous days' 10 min averaged time-windows has been used as a feature in the forecasting. All SVR parameters are kept the same for all predictions. As a result, for thirty-one out of thirty-five 10 min time-windows, IMF or IMF combinations approximate the real data better than using raw data in the prediction process. With the method we applied we approximate the next day's 10 min averaged power production with a maximum of 18% of error. Twenty-nine out of thirty-five time windows have been predicted with an error of less than 10%, and six of those are predicted with an error of less than 1%. With the results obtained in this study, we suggest that the EMD-based signal decomposition could be beneficial in wind power/speed forecasting by increasing accuracy.

References

1. Vindbrukskollen. https://vbk.lansstyrelsen.se/en. Accessed 19 July 2022
2. Abedi, H., Sarkar, S., Johansson, H.: Numerical modelling of neutral atmospheric boundary layer flow through heterogeneous forest canopies in complex terrain (a case study of a Swedish wind farm). Renewable Energy **180**, 806–828 (2021)
3. Altıntaş, A., Davidson, L., Peng, S.: A new approximation to modulation-effect analysis based on empirical mode decomposition. Phys. Fluids **31**(2), 025117 (2019)
4. Altıntaş, A., Davidson, L., Kostaras, G., Isaac, M.: The day-ahead forecasting of the passenger occupancy in public transportation by using machine learning. In: Martins, A.L., Ferreira, J.C., Kocian, A. (eds.) Intelligent Transport Systems. INTSYS 2021. Lecture Notes of the Institute for Computer Sciences, Social Informatics and Telecommunications Engineering, vol. 426, pp. 3–12. Springer, Cham (2022). https://doi.org/10.1007/978-3-030-97603-3_1
5. Archer, C.L., Jacobson, M.Z.: Evaluation of global wind power. J. Geophys. Res.: Atmospheres **110**(D12), D12110 (2005)
6. Hong, Y.Y., Yu, T.H., Liu, C.Y.: Hour-ahead wind speed and power forecasting using empirical mode decomposition. Energies **6**(12), 6137–6152 (2013)
7. Hu, X., Jaraitė, J., Kažukauskas, A.: The effects of wind power on electricity markets: A case study of the Swedish intraday market. Energy Econ. **96**, 105159 (2021)
8. Huang, N.E., et al.: The empirical mode decomposition and the Hilbert spectrum for nonlinear and non-stationary time series analysis. In: Proceedings of the Royal Society of London. Series A: Mathematical, Physical and Engineering Sciences **454**(1971), pp. 903–995 (1998)
9. Liu, K., Zhang, Y., Qin, L.: Erratum:"A novel combined forecasting model for short-term wind power prediction based on ensemble empirical mode decomposition and optimal virtual prediction". J. Renew. Sustain. Energy **8**, 013104 (2016)
10. Mauritzen, J.: Now or later? trading wind power closer to real time and how poorly designed subsidies lead to higher balancing costs. Energy J. **36**(4), 149–164 (2015)

11. Nava, N., Di Matteo, T., Aste, T.: Financial time series forecasting using empirical mode decomposition and support vector regression. Risks **6**(1), 7 (2018)

12. Piwko, R., Jordan, G.: Impacts of improved day-ahead wind forecasts on power grid operations: September 2011. Tech. rep., National Renewable Energy Lab. (NREL), Golden, CO (United States) (2011)

13. Premanode, B., Vongprasert, J., Toumazou, C.: Noise reduction for nonlinear non-stationary time series data using averaging intrinsic mode function. Algorithms **6**(3), 407–429 (2013)

14. Qiu, X., Suganthan, P.N., Amaratunga, G.A.: Short-term electricity price forecasting with empirical mode decomposition based ensemble kernel machines. Procedia Comput. Sci. **108**, 1308–1317 (2017)

15. Ren, Y., Suganthan, P., Srikanth, N.: Ensemble methods for wind and solar power forecasting-a state-of-the-art review. Renew. Sustain. Energy Rev. **50**, 82–91 (2015)

16. Rintamäki, T., Siddiqui, A.S., Salo, A.: Strategic offering of a flexible producer in day-ahead and intraday power markets. Eur. J. Oper. Res. **284**(3), 1136–1153 (2020)

17. Steen, D., et al.: Challenges of integrating solar and wind into the electricity grid. In: Systems Perspectives on Renewable Power, pp. 94–107 (2014)

Prediction of Risks Assessment in the Workplace Using Online Monitoring

Lucia Knapčíková[1]([✉]) [iD], Annamária Behúnová[2] [iD], Jozef Husár[1] [iD],
Rebeka Tauberová[1], and Matúš Martiček[1]

[1] Faculty of Manufacturing Technologies With a Seat in Prešov, Department of Industrial Engineering and Informatics, The Technical University of Košice, Bayerova 1, 080 01 Prešov, Slovak Republic
{lucia.knapcikova,jozef.husar,rebeka.tauberova}@tuke.sk,
matus.marticek@student.tuke.sk
[2] Faculty of Mining, Ecology, Process Control and Geotechnologies, Institute of Earth Resources, Technical University of Košice, Košice, Slovak Republic
annamaria.behunova@tuke.sk

Abstract. The digitization of technological processes in enterprises is rapidly changing the world of work and requires new and up-to-date solutions in occupational health and safety (OSH). The European Agency for Safety and Health at Work (EU-OSHA) provide information to policymakers, researchers and workers about the possible effects of digitization on OSH, so that they can take timely and effective measures to ensure the safety and protection of workers. Occupational health and safety are often poorly managed in micro and small enterprises, and employees are exposed to a greater risk of workplace injuries and occupational diseases. The paper deals with online monitoring of risk assessment in the injection moulding workplace and is key to creating healthy workplaces. However, conducting a risk assessment can be quite challenging, especially for micro and small businesses that may lack the resources or expertise to do it effectively.

Keywords: Monitoring · Communication · Circular Economy · Sustainability

1 Introduction

Safety and health protection at work can be defined as the state of the workplace, which ensures that in compliance with rules such as technological procedures, safety regulations, etc., a situation will not arise that would endanger workers' health [1]. To create safe work, in which the protection of the worker's health is to be observed, it is required to develop and implement a system of measures such as legislative, economic, social, organizational, technical, health and educational. [2] Despite the implementation of all available measures to increase safety, health protection and conscientious compliance with the organization's occupational safety and health policy (OSH) by employees, it does not exclude the occurrence of an undesirable situation that leads to occupational accidents [1, 2]. If such an undesirable situation occurs, it is necessary to proceed according to the applicable legislation [3].

© ICST Institute for Computer Sciences, Social Informatics and Telecommunications Engineering 2023
Published by Springer Nature Switzerland AG 2023. All Rights Reserved
J. L. Afonso et al. (Eds.): SESC 2022, LNICST 502, pp. 12–22, 2023.
https://doi.org/10.1007/978-3-031-33979-0_2

Hazard identification is the process of identifying whether a given hazard exists. This process also determines what the hazard can cause. The identified danger is then assessed, and one of the options is selected [3]:

1) interruption of the process due to a danger that is incompatible with the damage they can cause,
2) immediate adoption of corrective measures that eliminate or reduce threats arising from the hazard,
3) termination of the analysis due to negligible dangers,
4) continuation of risk identification.

The term threat means any activity that leads to the emergence of a dangerous situation. It represents a danger that causes negative phenomena such as injury or damage in a specific space and time in the machine-person-environment system [4].

The hazard identification stage is followed by the threat title and, at the same time, its analysis. This process represents the determination of threats that result from hazards and lead to an injury, damage or another negative phenomenon. Therefore, it is important to determine the course and method of potential negative risk in the machine-man-environment system. In this section, it is important to realize that one danger can cause more threats [2, 3].

Control measures for the identified threat [1, 2]:

1) Elimination - removal: introducing automated devices that reduce the manual work performed and eliminated threats.
2) Substitution - alternative: this measure is used if it is impossible to eliminate the threat. In such a case, possible options are sought to replace the materials, machines and equipment that are safer and eliminate the risk of injury or occupational disease.
3) Technical controls: they consist of the design of the workplace and the activities performed by the worker. An example can be technical noise control and the subsequent proposal of corrective measures such as anti-noise walls, covers and isolating employees from excessive noise.
4) Administrative regulation: represents measures, the content of which is the reworking of work procedures, introducing new strategies and determining the use of PPE.

1.1 The Risk Identification

It includes the process of identification, knowledge and assessment of existing, possible and emerging risks, which carry with them the probability of the occurrence of a negative phenomenon [1, 4].

The identification process must take risks into account, regardless of whether the given source of risk is under the organisation's control but also if the individual sources of risks and their causes are not obvious [5]. It must contain an assessment of the induced effects with consequences. It is important to consider the wide range of values, even if the individual sources of risks and their causes are not obvious [4]. It is also necessary to take into account what can happen and, at the same time, consider possible undesirable reasons and circumstances that indicate the consequences that could occur. All important causes and effects should be considered [5, 6] (Fig. 1).

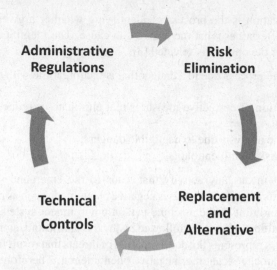

Fig. 1. The process of Online Monitoring [Authors own processing]

The process of identifying and assessing adverse events that lead to the creation and realization of risks, analysis of mechanisms leading to these situations, and assessment of the scope, size and probability of occurrence of any event that could harm the company "[6].

It consists of the following steps [4, 7]:

- determination of the assessed system,
- hazard identification,
- threat identification,
- determination of risks.

Monitoring is a tool to track almost everything - from the location of objects to the utilization of machines and the charging cycle of the battery of the transporting forklift - where such maintenance saves energy - to the list of people who are still on their way to work. Risk analysis is important in determining whether risks need to be addressed in a given chosen system and what method needs to be used to assess risk [6]. It provides information about individual sources of risk and also about positive or negative consequences and probabilities that may occur [7]. It has the task of identifying the factors that influence the values and, at the same time, their possibility. The risk is often expressed from a combination of consequences and probabilities [8]. In terms of the purpose of the analysis, available sources, information and data, the study can be qualitative, semi-quantitative or quantitative [7, 8].

2 Work Methodology

Digital technologies have brought new forms of employee management. Unlike previous forms of management that relied heavily on human supervision, AI workforce management relies on new management systems and tools that gather real-time data on worker behaviour from various sources [6]. The goal is to inform management and support automated or semi-automated decisions based on algorithms or more advanced forms of artificial intelligence [5]. Research in this area identifies and discusses the possibilities that these new systems provide for management based on artificial intelligence because if they are created and implemented transparently, and employees are informed and consulted, they can support decisions to improve health and safety in the workplace [6, 7]. In addition, the research maps and discusses challenges in the legal, regulatory, and ethical fields, as well as issues related to privacy and risks and concerns in the area of health and safety, especially about psychosocial risk factors that these new forms of monitoring and management of workers also cause [8, 9] (Fig. 2)

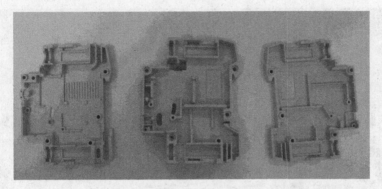

Fig. 2. The monitored samples of the final product [10].

Online monitoring and identification of risks at the injection moulding workplace was implemented in a company that focuses mainly on producing components for the electrical industry [10, 11]. The operation also uses other equipment designed for handling forms and moving material, such as a forklift and a gantry crane with a load capacity of up to 5000 kg [11]. A forklift is used for other injection moulding machines to change the mould. A very important task is also the drying of the material called granulate. The reservoirs of other injection moulding machines are filled manually, but before that, the granulate is dried in dryers that do not perform the function of automatic transfer of granulate to the reservoir [10]. It mainly concerns the production of mouldings of single and multi-pole circuit breakers, protectors, cam switches, and household electrical installation materials such as single and double 230V sockets, 400V sockets, switchboards, etc. [12] (Fig. 3).

3   Results and Discussion

The risk situations in the operation of injection moulding machines are the fall of the load and the slip - the fall of a person [10, 13]. They enter mainly using a forklift truck and filling dryers and hoppers of injection moulding machines [14]. These situations can seriously damage the health of workers (Fig. 4).

The following situation with a high level of risk is a slip - a person's fall, which most often occurs when filling the hoppers of dryers and injection moulding machines [15,

Fig. 3. The monitored products [10].

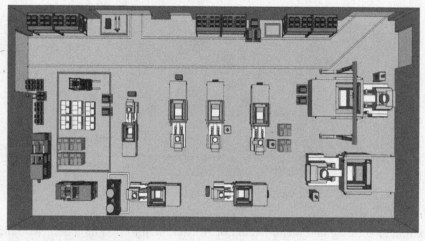

Fig. 4. Model of the current state of operation of injection moulding machines [10].

16]. To eliminate this risk, a model of preparation for filling these reservoirs with an active sensor using a bridge crane was created [17, 18] (Fig. 5).

Legend to Fig. 6

1. Preparation container
2. Eyelets for fastening the rope
3. A spring connected to a fixed part and a movable foot
4. The area of material (granules) coming out of the hopper
5. A foot of the proposed preparation

Legend to Fig. 7

1. Preparation for filling reservoirs
2. Middle piece for the upper part of the magazine
3. Reservoir

The mentioned preparation represents a simple mechanism. Its principle consists of filling the preparation with coarse material from a bag or dryer and subsequent transfer using a bridge crane above the level of the injection moulding tank [19, 20] (Fig. 8).

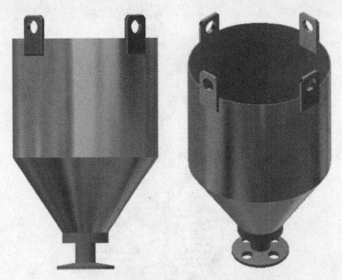

Fig. 5. Model of preparation for filling reservoirs [10].

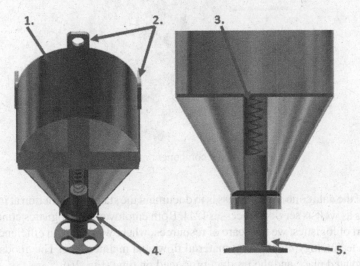

Fig. 6. The main parts of the preparation [10].

Legend to Fig. 9

1. The preparation is closed
2. The preparation is open

When lowering, the foot of the preparation rests on the intermediate piece of the upper part of the container, and the weight of the preparation and the filled granulate pushes the foot into the inner part, which partially opens the closing position [20, 21]. After opening, the granulate is poured directly into the hopper of the injection moulding machine. When raised again, the spring pushes the foot outwards, closing the closing

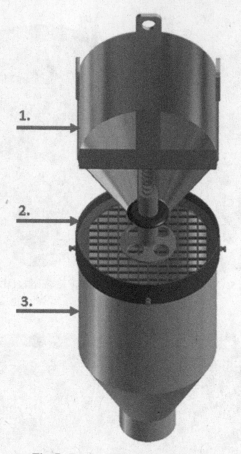

Fig. 7. Basic component mode [10].

part. Part of the data collection process is to document the state of production at individual workplaces as well as service processes [21]. Both employers and logistics contribute to this. As part of logistics, we take care of resources, where we deal with efficiency, health and safety, technology monitoring, material flow, and maintenance. The goods must be at the designated place and the product produced on time (Fig. 10).

Fig. 8. The proposed spacer [10].

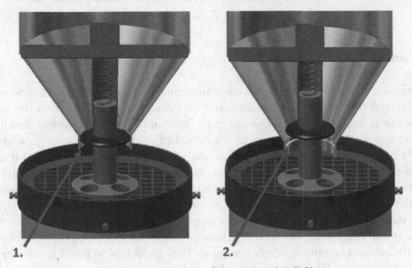

Fig. 9. The principle of the preparation [10].

Fig. 10. The workstation view

4 Conclusion

The research aimed to predict, monitor and subsequently minimize risks when working in the injection moulding department based on theoretical principles from the safety and health protection field. Part of the main activities of every company should be creating safe work at the workplace, which should ensure the protection of the employers' r's health. An important condition is the identification of dangers, and threats, the definition of risk levels and subsequent solutions for risk elimination. To carry out the risk identification, it was important to characterize the production and the detailed activities of individual workers where there are potential dangers and threats. Operational safety is also one of the company's priorities. Increasing production, movement of equipment, employees, visitors brings various dangerous situations. Digital technologies also increase security of whole company. They know how to guard the authorized use of technology and the authorization of the operator; they prevent collision situations between vehicles and pedestrians. This will prevent damage, injuries and unnecessary costs associated with accidents and maintenance.

Acknowledgements. This work was supported by the projects VEGA 1/0268/22, KEGA 038TUKE-4/2022 granted by the Ministry of Education, Science, Research and Sport of the Slovak Republic.

References

1. Periša, M., Cvitić, I., Peraković, D., Husnjak, S.: Beacon technology for real-time informing the traffic network users about the environment. Transport **34**, 373–382 (2019). https://doi.org/10.3846/transport.2019.10402
2. Nagyova, A., Pacaiova, H., Markulik, S., et al.: Design of a Model for Risk Reduction in Project Management in Small and Medium-Sized Enterprises. Symetry-Basel, vol. 13 (5) (2021). https://doi.org/10.3390/sym13050763
3. Periša, M., Kuljanić, T.M., Cvitić, I., Kolarovszki, P.: Conceptual model for informing user with innovative smart wearable device in industry 4.0. Wireless Netw. **27**(3), 1615–1626 (2019). https://doi.org/10.1007/s11276-019-02057-9
4. Straka, M., Khouri, S., et al.: Utilization of computer simulation for waste separation design as a logistics system. Int. J. Simul. Modelling **17**(4), 83–596 (2018). https://doi.org/10.2507/IJSIMM17(4)444
5. Gou, Z., Yamaguchi, S., e al.: Analysis of various security issues and challenges in cloud computing environment: a survey. In: Identity Theft: Breakthroughs in Research and Practice, pp. 221–247. IGI global (2017)
6. Prandi, C., Nunes, N., Ribeiro, M., Nisi, V.: Enhancing sustainable mobility awareness by exploiting multi-sourced data: the case study of the Madeira Islands. Sustainable Internet and ICT for Sustainability (SustainIT), Funchal, pp. 1–5 (2017)
7. Hugos, M.H., Hulitzky, D.: Business in the cloud: what every business needs to know about cloud computing. John Wiley & Sons, p. 139 (2010)
8. Lee, C.K.M., Zhang, S.Z., Ng, K.K.H.: Development of an industrial Internet of things suite for smart factory towards re-industrialization. Adv. Manuf. **5**(4), 335–343 (2017). https://doi.org/10.1007/s40436-017-0197-2
9. Globa, L., Kurdecha, V., Ishchenko,I., Zakharchuk, A., Kunieva, N.: The intellectual IoT-system for monitoring the base station quality of service. In: 2018 IEEE International Black Sea Conference on Communications and Networking (BlackSeaCom), Batumi, pp. 1–5 (2018). https://doi.org/10.1109/BlackSeaCom.2018.8433715
10. Foriš, J.: Identification of risks at the workplace of injection pressers in the selected company. Technical University of Košice, Thesis (2017)
11. Catini, A., et al.: Development of a sensor node for remote monitoring of plants. Sensors **19**, 4865 (2019)
12. Giordano, M.R., et al.: From low-cost sensors to high-quality data: a summary of challenges and best practices for effectively calibrating low-cost particulate matter mass sensors. J. Aerosol Sci. **158**, 105833 (2021). https://doi.org/10.1016/j.jaerosci.2021.105833
13. Fözö, L., et al.: Simulation aspects of adaptive control design for small turbojet engines, in Intelligent Engineering Systems, (IEEE Industrial Electronics Society, Budapešt (Mad'arsko), 2019), pp. 101–106. ISBN 978-1-7281-1212-
14. Chen, X.Y., Jin, Z.G.: Research on key technology and applications for internet of things. Phys. Procedia **33**, 561–566 (2012)
15. Vegsoova, O., Khouri, S., Straka, M., Rosova, A., Kacmary, P., Betus, M.: Using technical means and logistics principle applications to solve ecological water course accidents. Pol. J. Environ. Stud. **28**(5), 3875–3883 (2019)
16. Lamont, G.B., Slear, J.N., Melendez, K.: UAV swarm mission planning and routing using multi-objective evolutionary algorithms. Presented at the 2007 IEEE Symposium on Computational Intelligence in Multi-Criteria Decision-Making (2007)
17. de Melo, V.V., Banzhaf, W.: Drone Squadron Optimization: a novel self-adaptive algorithm for global numerical optimization. Neural Comput. Appl. **30**(10), 3117–3144 (2017). https://doi.org/10.1007/s00521-017-2881-3

18. Drozd, W., Leśniak, A.: Ecological wall systems as an element of sustainable developmentcost issues. Sustainability **10**(7), 2234 (2018)
19. Marto, A., Goncalves, A.: Mobile AR: User Evaluation in a Cultural Heritage Context.Applied Sciences-Basel, vol. 9 (24), 5454 (2019)
20. Mesároš, P., Mandičák, T.: Information systems for material flow management in construction processes. In: IOP Conferences Series: Materials Science and Engineering, pp. 1–5 (2015)
21. Trebuňa, P., et al.: 3D scanning as a modern technology for creating 3D models. Acta Tecnología **6**(1), 21–24 (2020)

Study of Hardware and Software Resources for Mobile Applications of Immersive Technologies in Manufacturing

Jozef Husár[1]([✉]) [iD], Lucia Knapčíková[1] [iD], and Justyna Trojanowska[2] [iD]

[1] Faculty of Manufacturing Technologies With a Seat in Prešov, Department of Industrial Engineering and Informatics, Technical University of Košice, Bayerova 1, 080 01 Prešov, Slovak Republic
{jozef.husar,lucia.knapcikova}@tuke.sk
[2] Faculty of Mechanical Engineering, Department of Production Engineering, Poznan University of Technology, Piotrowo Street 3, 61-138 Poznan, Poland
justyna.trojanowska@put.poznan.pl

Abstract. Immersive technologies (IT) create different experiences by combining the physical world with digital or simulated reality. Virtual augmented and mixed reality are the main types of immersive technologies. Since the beginning of the millennium, VR, AR and MR technologies have experienced rapid growth with significant research publications in technology and science. However, the engineering community has only minimally implemented these technologies so far. One of the challenges mechanical engineers face in understanding and using extended reality (ER) combining VR, AR, MR is the lack of hardware and software requirements specification. This document provides a literature review on mobile applications of immersive technologies in engineering production. A historical overview of the concept of applications used in industry was gradually created. Subsequently, the hardware and software pro-resources used for XR in production are presented. The article is intended to find a good fit between XR hardware and software solutions based on professional and technical knowledge in engineering fields.

Keywords: Augmented reality · Automotive industry · Visualization · Personalization

1 Introduction

The term "Extended Reality (XR)" refers to the growing category of immersive technologies that encompasses Virtual Reality (VR), Augmented Reality (AR), and Mixed Reality (MR). As the popularity of virtual experiences continues to rise, particularly in response to the pandemic, XR technologies are becoming increasingly accessible to a wider audience. Many progressive industrial enterprises are already testing immersive technologies in their operations. The reason is the significant potential of technology

J. L. Afonso et al. (Eds.): SESC 2022, LNICST 502, pp. 23–34, 2023.
https://doi.org/10.1007/978-3-031-33979-0_3

to help people do their jobs better and more efficiently. With the rapid development of simulation technologies, computer graphics and human-computer interaction technologies, VR, AR and MR will gain more application domains. The market involving these technologies has grown incredibly. VR, AR and MR are used in several industries and concepts, from the manufacturing industry to consumers. It is the manufacturing industry that offers added value in countless applications. XR technologies such as AR, MR, and VR bring new solutions to industrial production by creating a blended environment where virtual and real objects can interact. These immersive technologies enhance the interaction between people by integrating digital technology into physical space. AR, MR, and VR are utilized when replicating reality is difficult or costly. Each technology has its distinct characteristics, with VR offering a completely virtual experience, AR adding virtual elements to the real world, and MR allowing interaction with these virtual elements in real-world scenarios. In recent years, VR and AR have become more accessible to individual users, but MR is still primarily used by large companies. While VR and AR can be used on mobile devices, MR requires more computing power.

1.1 VR, AR, MR: Conceptions

The convergence of digital and physical elements characterizes VR, AR, and MR. These cutting-edge technologies revolutionize human-computer interaction by seamlessly blending the virtual and real realms, delivering unprecedented experiences. Due to society's increasing demand for innovation and the investments and efforts of technology and mass media companies, these three realities are becoming more integral parts of our daily lives. To distinguish between them, it is crucial to comprehend their underlying concepts.

Virtual Reality (VR)
Virtual Reality (VR) is a computer-generated, fully immersive experience that consists of either computer-created environments and objects or 360-degree videos. To be considered VR, a program must completely alter the user's surroundings, creating a simulated environment that the user can interact with and perceive through a combination of sensory information [1]. The goal of VR is to accurately display and manipulate spatial models and scenes, recreating part of the real world with its laws and movements in 3D space, all in real-time. VR uses computer graphics and computer science techniques to achieve this and provides content through a head-mounted display (HMD) or headset. The content is purely digital and the user is transported to a new 3D digital environment, separate from the real world [2].

Augmented Reality (AR)
"Augmented Reality" is a term that describes a technology that combines real-world and computer-generated content in real-time. It leverages the advancements made in Virtual Reality (VR) and enables interaction between the physical and virtual realms [3]. It is the projection or adding a layer of digital content to a real physical environment in real time. Augmented reality integrates digital components through applications on mobile devices into the real world, and digital content is visible through special AR glasses or using a tablet/smartphone, stationary screens, projection devices and other

technologies [4]. AR, as defined by [5], is a technology that merges the real world with computer graphics and enables real-time interaction between objects. It has the capability to track objects, recognize objects and images, and provide real-time data and contextual information. Augmented reality has different types that fall into two categories. These include brand-based augmented reality, and brand-free augmented reality.

Mixed Reality (MR)

Mixed Reality (MR) is a technology that allows digital and real objects to interact and coexist in real-time. The user can manipulate digital objects, which then react as real, physical objects would. This technology is also known as hybrid reality and requires a more powerful MR headset and processing power compared to VR or AR. MR brings together various technologies into a single wearable device [6]. The objective of MR is to achieve a seamless fusion of the real and digital realms through the stimulation of the user's senses and incorporating digital information into their line of sight. The difficulty in MR technology lies in registering virtual and real content accurately in real-time and presenting computer-generated 3D graphics. Currently, efforts are focused on enhancing tracking capabilities, particularly for mobile devices.

1.2   VR, AR, MR: Development

The origin of immersive technologies dates back to 1838 when charles wheatstone invented the stereoscope [8]. This technology was used to create 3D images. Since then, these technologies have developed at a rapid pace but have remained a subject of interest until today. This chapter presents the appearance and development of VR, AR and MR.

VR Development

Virtual Reality (VR) as we know it has evolved over several decades due to advancements in technology and more affordable high-performance computing processors. Key milestones in VR's development include:

- Sensorama (1960–1962) by Morton Heilig, the first attempt at VR with a multi-sensory simulator that played pre-recorded films with 3D display, stereo sound, fans, scent generator, and vibrating chair.
- The Ultimate Display (1965) proposal by Ivan Sutherland, combining interactive graphics, force feedback, sound, smell, and taste.
- "Sword of Damocles" (1967) - the first VR system with hardware, believed to be the first head-tracking HMD.
- GROPE (1971) - a force-feedback system prototype at the University of North Carolina.
- VIDEOPLACE (1975) by Myron Krueger, an artificial reality system projecting users' silhouettes captured by cameras onto a large screen for interaction.
- VCASS (1982) - Thomas Furness developed an advanced flight simulator using an HMD to display targeting information and extend the view from the window.
- VIVED (1984) - NASA Ames built a Virtual Visual Environment Display using standard stereoscopic monochrome HMD technology.
- VPL - produced the first commercially available VR devices, the DataGlove (1985) and Eyephone HMD (1988).

- BOOM - a box with two CRT monitors viewed through eye holes, allowing users to move around in a virtual world with a mechanical arm tracking their position and orientation.
- UNC Walkthrough Project (1980s) - an architectural walkthrough application at the University of North Carolina using HMDs, optical trackers, and Pixel-Plane graphics engine to enhance VR experience.
- Virtual Wind Tunnel (early 1990s) - developed at NASA Ames, this system allowed for flow field study using BOOM and DataGlove.
- CAVE (1992) - a high-quality visualization system that projects stereoscopic images onto a room's walls, providing better resolution and wider field of view than HMD-based systems.

Prior to the emergence of commercial high-end VR systems, such as the Samsung Oculus Rift and HTC Vive, in the early 2010s, VR technology was limited to specialized researchers and came with a hefty price tag, hindering its commercial viability [10, 11]. While these commercial VR systems are connected to high-end PCs, providing users with high refresh rates, immersive environments, and multiple interaction options, they are confined to a limited space near the PC and require significant computing power, which can be expensive [12]. A more budget-friendly VR option is VR-compatible mobile devices (smartphones), which may not offer the same quality VR experience as the high-end systems but are more affordable due to their lower computing power [13].

AR Development
In the early 1990s, augmented reality gained significant attention and became the subject of numerous research projects due to its immense potential. The history of Augmented Reality (AR) includes the following milestones:

- 1990 - Tom Caudell was the first to use the term "Augmented Reality".
- Virtual Fixtures (1992) - An early AR system developed by Louis Rosenburg for the USAF Armstrong Research Laboratory, allowing military personnel to control machines.
- Dancing in Cyberspace (1994) - A theatrical production with acrobats dancing with virtual objects projected on stage.
- NASA X-38 spacecraft (1999) - Used a hybrid synthetic vision system with AR technology for navigation.
- ARToolKit (2000) - Open source software library for AR development.
- 1st & Ten (2003) - Improved graphics system for sports with overlaid graphics.
- Esquire magazine (2009) - Used AR in print media for the first time.
- Volkswagen's MARTA (2013) - AR app for technicians with detailed instructions.
- Google Glass (2014) - AR glasses connecting to internet via smartphone Bluetooth.
- Microsoft's HoloLens (n.d.) - Advanced AR headset running on Windows 10.
- IKEA Place (2017) - AR app for virtual tryout of home decor before purchase.
- ARKit (2017) - Added to iOS 11 by Apple for quick AR app creation.

MR Development
In their 1994 paper "A Taxonomy of Mixed Reality Visual Displays," researchers Paul Milgram and Fumio Kishino introduced the concept of MR. They described a "virtuality

continuum" that connects the real and virtual worlds. Originally, Milgram and Kishino envisioned MR mainly in terms of visual displays, but it has since expanded to encompass information perceived by other senses as well [14]. MR is a combination of VR and AR technology. It gained popularity after the introduction of Microsoft HoloLens. However, it's still hard to find many options that offer a true "MR" experience. Among vendors experimenting with mixed reality, information about how the technology works is scarce. In 2018, Magic Leap announced the launch of its first mixed reality glasses, the Magic Leap One Creator Edition. The kit was sold in six US cities and cost $2,295[15]. In 2021, Magic Leap introduced the second version of its headset. Unlike VR, Magic Leap's AR headsets project digital 3D objects on top of the real world. The new headset is primarily intended for corporate use and has a wider field of vision [16].

2 Research

Today, XR technologies have gained great popularity and many application domains. One of the most important areas of their use is education. For example, Google Expeditions interactive technology allows students to sit in their classroom and immerse themselves in virtual worlds. Similarly, applications such as Unimersiv fully engage students in a virtual environment where they can even hear sounds, such as people speaking foreign languages, etc., which has been proven to help with learning and development. 9 out of 10 UK teachers acknowledge that XR technologies would benefit their teaching [16] (Fig. 1).

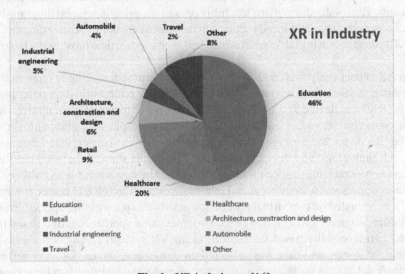

Fig. 1. XR in Industry [16]

Aside from education, XR technologies are also applied in fields such as design, architecture, and engineering. Virtual reality has many potential uses, one of which is allowing architects to create 1:1 scale models of their projects, which they can then examine, manipulate, and test before actual construction begins. Automotive engineers can also use VR to design and develop new cars and engines, saving costs by avoiding the creation of multiple physical prototypes. Furniture manufacturers are now utilizing AR technology to let customers virtually try out furniture in their homes prior to purchasing. XR provides an innovative way for people to immerse themselves in various new scenarios through simulation technology, and offers practical solutions to contemporary challenges.

Examples of XR Applications in Manufacturing:
In the field of manufacturing, XR has shown potential for enhancing maintenance processes. A case study was conducted in a Swedish snus company to explore the benefits of a wearable AR system for maintenance tasks. The study involved developing an AR system for a toolbox and testing it with 17 experts at a maintenance fair in Sweden. The results of the study indicated that AR can support maintenance in manufacturing. However, designing AR interfaces requires more attention, as they are different from traditional 2D interfaces. It is crucial to have a good understanding of the production activity and available AR technologies before implementing an AR system to ensure optimal results [17].

An XR application was demonstrated at a drone factory in Sweden's National Test Laboratory. The factory relied mainly on traditional operator support like paper instructions and monitor-based illustrations [18]. The study explored the new possibilities of using an AR system to present instructions, including structural and active diagram-based instructions, and incorporating tablets and Microsoft HoloLens. The AR mounting support system was tested with two control methods: touchscreen buttons and voice commands. The results showed that assembly operations using functional diagram-based instructions were faster and more accurate than those using the structural diagram approach. The operators using tablets performed better on average than those using HoloLens [19].

An AR impact study was conducted at a Swedish firm specializing in indoor climate and ventilation solutions. The study aimed to examine the effects of AR on order picking using a HoloLens device and Unity3D software. Five company representatives tested the AR system on two orders, each with 12 or 14 items. Despite all participants correctly selecting the items, the average selection time was longer than expected due to user habits, AR limitations, and device limitations. The results showed the potential for AR to enhance order picking, despite the challenges posed by new wearable technology [20].

In another study at a Swedish global automotive company's R&D center, the impact of VR was evaluated on two virtual production activities: spot welding operator training and product design review. The study used two interaction approaches: BHI (hand tracking) and CBI (controller-based interaction) in the VR system. 22 engineers tested and evaluated the system and data was collected on immersion, interaction, and autonomy to compare the effects on the user experience. Results showed that hand tracking and synchronized visualization received higher preferences as they provided a more realistic experience and increased immersion. However, hand interaction with virtual objects proved to be more difficult than controller-based interaction. The study highlighted that XR technology brings new solutions and potential improvements but also new challenges that may hinder its widespread adoption in the industry [21].

3 HW and SW Tools for XR Application in the Manufacturing

3.1 HW Tool for VR, AR, MR Applications

Through the years, XR technology has advanced, leading to the development of increasingly sophisticated devices that are also smaller and more user-friendly. The devices differ in terms of appearance, weight, operating mode, field of view (FOV), and frames per second (FPS) capabilities [22].

For any XR system, a display screen is required to project virtual content. The FOV of the screen determines the visible area for the user, affecting the amount of virtual information that can be displayed. Ideally, the screen used in XR technologies should have a similar FOV as human eyes (114° horizontally) [23] to provide a more immersive experience and display important information effectively. However, currently available screens have varying FOVs, with VR headsets offering a wider FOV ranging from 90° to 110° (e.g. HP Reverb (G1), Oculus Quest, HTC Vive Cosmos) and some advanced models offering up to 200° (e.g. Pimax Vision 8K X).

Another important parameter is the FPS, which is the frequency of displaying successive images on the screen [23]. Higher FPS results in smoother content movement. Although FPS is important in AR or MR systems, it is more critical in VR systems, where users are fully immersed in a computer-generated environment. A recommended FPS for VR systems is 90 fps to avoid motion jitter and motion sickness, while AR or MR systems require 30–60 fps. Note that FPS is determined by both hardware and software.

The following listed HW tools for XR application in the manufacturing industry are the most promising and are most commonly used [21]:

HTC Vive
The HTC Vive is a VR headset created by HTC in collaboration with Valve, a video game developer. It boasts a high-res display of 2160 x 1200 with a refresh rate of 90Hz and a 110-degree FOV [26].Despite its advanced technology, the Vive is lightweight, weighing just over half a kilogram. It requires a powerful computer to run, with over 70 sensors such as a gyroscope, accelerometer, and laser position sensors providing a room-scale experience. The Vive also has a pro version that features improved resolution of 2880 x 1600 and wireless capabilities [24].

Oculus Rift
The original version of the headset was introduced in 2016 and had many similarities with the Vive, including its resolution and refresh rate, but lacked hand controls and room-scale capabilities. The Oculus Touch, a handheld controller system, was later released to provide a room-scale alternative to the Vive [27]. The Oculus Touch kit includes a headset and the controller. It also requires a relatively powerful computer, similar to the HTC Vive.

Microsoft Hololens
The Microsoft Hololens, noted as the preferred option for AR/MR in manufacturing, boasts a 2–3 h battery life and operates as a standalone device, eliminating the need for

a computer connection. Its 3D content is created by two light sensors and holographic lenses, producing a total resolution of 2.3 million light points. The device is equipped with an Inertial Measurement Unit, four cameras for environmental processing, an RGB camera, and a depth camera for mapping and merging the real and virtual worlds. Other features include four microphones, eye-tracking, gesture input, surround sound, and voice support [29].

Mobile Headset
Contrarily to the dedicated XR hardware mentioned earlier, devices like Samsung Gear VR, Google Daydream, and Google Cardboard are not standalone XR devices. These are plastic or cardboard head-mounted displays that depend on the display of a mobile phone. The major difference between these mobile XR solutions lies in their compatibility, ergonomics, and build quality. They are generally more affordable and portable, only needing a mobile phone instead of a computer. However, their tracking capabilities are limited due to the use of the phone's internal sensors and gyroscopes instead of advanced tracking hardware found in high-end headsets like the Oculus Rift and HTC Vive [31]. Another disadvantage is the low frame rate, with a recommended 90 Hz for a smooth user experience [32], which is difficult to achieve with a mobile phone. Mobile AR has the potential to improve project documentation comprehension and usability through visualizing preliminary studies and monitoring the manufacturing process [33]. However, it also has limitations such as poor alignment with the surrounding environment and a lack of a motion controller in some cases [34, 35]. Specialized AR devices such as the Microsoft Hololens are preferred in the construction phase due to these limitations.

3.2 SW Tools for VR, AR, and MR Applications

In production, various software are used to develop XR systems, either based on open-source platforms or commercial software. Open-source platforms offer more customization but require programming skills, while commercial software is user-friendly and easy to use with pre-existing XR features. However, the ability to try out new XR features is limited, as it depends on the software's updates [21].

Open development platforms
Unity3D [36] and Unreal Engine [37] are two of the most widely used open platforms that support XR technologies. These platforms have large and active communities that have developed fast-changing plugins that the manufacturing industry can quickly implement for custom XR development. Unity3D has gained recognition in the production industry through partnerships with top manufacturers globally, while Unreal Engine is well-known for its ability to produce photorealistic visualizations with ease.

Commercial SW platforms
The popularity of XR technology has led to its incorporation into commercial software used in manufacturing. XR experiences can be created using either open development platforms or commercial software. Open platforms offer customization but require software engineering skills, while commercial software is user-friendly but limited in exploring new XR features [38]. In the manufacturing industry, Siemens Plant Simulation supports VR for assembly line design analysis and maintenance training for steam

turbines [39]. Autodesk VRED is used for creating 3D product visualizations, virtual prototypes and VR, mainly in the automotive industry [40]. The latest version of ABB Robot Studio has improved its VR capabilities for better robotic system workspace [41]. Vuforia Studio enables rapid AR app development for operator support and training [42, 43]. Revizto is a software solution for real-time collaboration and coordination issues in AEC projects, with a focus on BIM [44]. It enables all project teams to work together on a single model, ensuring accurate and efficient collaboration. Revizto converts BIM and CAD models from popular tools like Trimble SketchUp, Autodesk Revit, and Autodesk AutoCAD into VR environments that can be navigated with Oculus and HTC Vive [45].

Atensi offers game-based learning solutions through interactive simulations of real-world scenarios, particularly in training and risk task simulations in the construction industry [46]. Dimension10, like Revizto, focuses on seamless BIM to VR and cloud storage. It supports popular BIM software from Autodesk and Solidworks, allowing multiple participants to collaborate in a scalable virtual space [47].

Trimble SiteVision is different from the other software mentioned in that it offers an AR experience instead of VR. With this software, users can visualize a construction site in the future or view what's underground, using Trimble's GNSS (Global Navigation Satellite System) hardware, which is connected to the user's phone or tablet [48]. Unlike the other software, which prioritize functionality over design, Trimble SiteVision provides an AR experience that enables users to see real-life construction sites.

4   Conclusion

As the manufacturing industry transforms digitally, XR technology is seen as the cornerstone for Industry 4.0. XR, in its forms of AR, MR, and VR, has transformed the interaction between users and computer systems. Initially, XR systems were limited by hardware and software constraints, making them costly and purpose-built. However, with technological advancements, XR systems are now more affordable and flexible, becoming as accessible as mainstream computer hardware. Different levels of virtuality offer pros and cons for specific tasks. For example, VR systems provide an immersive virtual environment but require more complex modeling, while AR systems can display additional information easily, but may face challenges with object tracking. Even within the same level of virtuality, there are varying hardware and software specifications. Wireless VR solutions offer mobility but have lower computing power and shorter operating times. Choosing the right XR solution for manufacturing activities requires expertise as XR devices vary in appearance and technical characteristics, such as weight, operating mode, field of view, and frames per second. Finding a match between XR and manufacturing requires a deep understanding of both. Today's XR headsets have a wide FOV - about 90–110 degrees, and some advanced models even have a FOV of 200 degrees. While for AR or MR systems, an FPS of 30–60 frames/s would be sufficient, for VR systems, an FPS of 90 frames/s is recommended. In the manufacturing industry, the most used hardware is HTC Vive, Oculus Rift, Microsoft Hololens and mobile headsets, but they have their disadvantages related to the performance of mobile devices. As for the software for XR, usually, this software is based on an open development platform, such as Unity3D and Unreal Engine, or is commercial, such as Plant Simulation, Autodesk

VRED, ABB Robot Studio, Vuforia Studio, Revizto, Atensi, Dimension10, Trimble SiteVision. Of course, the choice of hardware and software depends on the area and purpose of the XR implementation.

Acknowledgements. This work was supported by the projects VEGA 1/0268/22, KEGA 038TUKE-4/2022 granted by the Ministry of Education, Science, Research and Sport of the Slovak Republic.

Article is the result of the Project implementation: Development of excellent research capacities in the field of additive technologies for the Industry of the 21st century, ITMS: 313011BWN5, supported by the Operational Program Integrated Infrastructure funded by the ERDF.

References

1. Gatial, P.: Virtual reality. http://edu.fmph.uniba.sk/~winczer/SocialneAspekty/GatialVirtua lnaRealita.htm. Accessed 03 Nov 2022
2. The ultimate VR, AR, MR guide. https://www.aniwaa.com/guide/vr-ar/ultimate-vr-ar-mr-guide/. Accessed 03 Nov 2022
3. Wirth, W., Hartmann, T., Böcking, S., et al.: A process model of the formation of spatial presence experiences. Media Psychol. **9**, 493–525 (2007). https://doi.org/10.1080/152132 60701283079
4. Grubert, J., Langlotz, T., Zollmann S., et al.: Towards pervasive augmented reality: context-awareness in augmented reality. In: IEEE Transactions on Visualization and Computer Graphics, vol. 23, no. 6, pp. 1706–1724 (2017). https://doi.org/10.1109/TVCG.2016.2543720
5. Blimber, O.: Spatial augmented reality: merging real and virtual worlds. A K Peters, Wellesley (2005)
6. Mazuryk, T., Gervautz, M.: Virtual Reality—History, Applications, Technology and Future. TU Wien University, Vienna, Austia (1996)
7. Milgram, P., Takemura, H., Utsumi, A., Kishino, F.: Augmented reality: a class of displays on the reality-virtuality continuum. In: Das, H. (ed.) Telemanipulator and Telepresence Technologies, pp. 282–292 (1995). https://doi.org/10.1117/12.197321
8. Forrest, C.: Infographic: the history of AR and VR, and what the future holds. https://www.techrepublic.com/article/infographic-the-history-of-ar-and-vr-and-what-the-future-holds/. Accessed 04 Nov 2022
9. Poetker, B., (2019). A brief history of augmented reality. https://www.g2.com/articles/his tory-of-augmented-reality. Accessed 04 Nov 2022
10. Zinchenko, Y., Khoroshikh, P., Sergievich, A., et al.: Virtual reality is more efficient in learning human heart anatomy especially for subjects with low baseline knowledge. In: New Ideas in Psychology, vol. 59, no. 100786 (2020). https://doi.org/10.1016/j.newideapsych.2020.100786
11. Carruth, D.: Virtual reality for education and workforce training. In: Proceedings of the 15th International Conference on Emerging eLearning Technologies and Applications (ICETA), Stary Smokovec, Slovakia, 26–27 October (2017). https://doi.org/10.1109/ICETA.2017.810 2472
12. Radianti, J., Majchrzak, T., Fromm, J., et al.: A systematic review of immersive virtual reality applications for higher education: design elements, lessons learned, and research agenda. In: Computer Education, vol. 147, no. 103778 (2020). https://doi.org/10.1016/j.compedu.2019. 103778
13. Mazuryk, T., Gervautz, M.: Virtual reality history, applications, technology and future. Institute of Computer Graphics Vienna University of Technology, Austria. p. 72. (1999)

14. Milgram, P., Kishino F.: A taxonomy of mixed reality visual displays. In: IEICE Transactions on Information Systems, Vol E77-D, no. 12, pp.1321–1329 (1994)
15. Kretsu, C.: Timeline: how virtual, augmented and mixed reality evolved. https://vc.ru/fut ure/44433-hronologiya-kak-razvivalas-virtualnaya-dopolnennaya-i-smeshannaya-realosti. Accessed 02 Nov 2022
16. What Is the future of XR?. https://www.hire-intelligence.co.uk/the-future-of-xr/. Accessed 02 Nov 2022
17. Kraft, H., Mäki, H., Bengtsson, J., et al.: Augmented reality in preventive maintenance. Bachelor thesis, Dept. Ind. Mater. Sci., Chalmers Univ. Technol., Gothenburg, Sweden, (2018). https://hdl.handle.net/20.500.12380/255323. Accessed 04 Nov 2022
18. Hansson, O., Nadum, O.: Model based operator instructions using AR-technology, M.S. thesis, Department of Industrial and Materials Science Chalmers University of Technology Gothenburg, Sweden (2019). https://hdl.handle.net/20.500.12380/300753. Accessed 04 Nov 2022
19. Agrawala, M., Phan, D., Heiser, J., Haymaker, J., et al: Designing effective step-by-step assembly instructions. ACM Trans. Graph. 22(3), 828–837 (2003). https://doi.org/10.1145/882262.882352
20. Mahmutovic, A., Andreasson, A., Söderström, L.: Effektivisering av plockprocessen i lager med hjälp AV AR, Bachelor thesis, Department of Industrial and Materials Science Chalmers University of Technology Gothenburg, Sweden (2018). https://hdl.handle.net/20.500.12380/255328. Accessed 03 Nov 2022
21. Gong, L., Fast-Berglund, A., Johansson, B.: A framework for extended reality system development in manufacturing. IEEE Access 9(1), 24796–24813 (2021). https://doi.org/10.1109/ACCESS.2021.3056752
22. Gong, L.: Developing extended reality systems for the manufacturing industry. Thesis for the Degree of Doctor of Philosophy, Department of Industrial and Materials Science Chalmers University of Technology Gothenburg, Sweden (2020)
23. Howard I., Rogers, B.: Binocular vision and stereopsis. New York, NY, USA: Oxford University Press (1996). https://doi.org/10.1093/acprof:oso/9780195084764.001.0001
24. Kaushal, V.: Exploratory study: implementation and applications of extended reality. Master's Thesis, Faculty of Science and Technology, University of Stavanger, Department of Mechanical and Structural Engineering and Materials Science (2019)
25. Martindale, J.: Oculus Rift vs. HTC Vive. https://www.digitaltrends.com/virtual-reality/ocu lus-rift-vs-htc-vive/. Accessed 04 Nov 2022
26. Jaffrey Van Camp: Review: HTC Vive Pro. https://www.wired.com/review/review-htc-vive-pro/. Accessed 04 Nov 2022
27. Lang, B.: Oculus Rift and HTC Vive Roomscale Dimensions Compared. https://www.roadtovr.com/oculus-touch-and-htc-vive-roomscale-dimensions-compared-versus-vs-visual ized/. Accessed 04 Nov 2022
28. Burns, Ch.: Oculus Rift just cut price for 3rd time this year. https://www.slashgear.com/ocu lus-rift-just-cut-price-for-3rd-time-this-year-11503613/. Accessed 03 Nov 2022
29. Evans, G., Miller, J., Pena, M.I., MacAllister, A., et al.: Evaluating the Microsoft Hololens through an Augmented Reality assembly application. Degraded Environ.: Sens., Process., Display 10197, 101970V (2017). https://doi.org/10.1117/12.2262626
30. Manufacturers are successfully using mixed reality today. https://www.themanufacturer.com/articles/manufacturers-are-successfully-using-mixed-reality-today/. Accessed 04 Nov 2022
31. Painter, L.: Daydream VR vs HTC Vive & Oculus Rift | Mobile VR vs PC VR. https://www.techadvisor.com/review/daydream-vr-vs-htc-vive-oculus-rift-mobile vr-vs-pc-vr-3647738/. Accessed 03 Nov 2022

32. Schlueter, J., Baiotto, H., Hoover, M., et al.: Best practices for cross-platform virtual reality development. Degraded Environ.: Sensing, Process. Display **10197**, 1019709 (2017). https://doi.org/10.1117/12.2262718

33. Meža, S., Turk, Z., Dolenc, M.: Measuring the potential of augmented reality in civil engineering. Adv. Eng. Softw. **90**, 1–10 (2015). https://doi.org/10.1016/j.advengsoft.2015.06.005

34. Heinzel, A., Azhar, S., Nadeem, A.: Uses of augmented reality technology during construction phase. In: 9th International Conference of Construction in the Twenty-first Century (CITC9), 5. – 7. marca 2017, Dubaj (2017)

35. Kaščak, J., Husár, J., Knapčíková, L., Trojanowska, J., Ivanov, V.: Conceptual use of augmented reality in the maintenance of manufacturing facilities. In: Trojanowska, J., Kujawińska, A., Machado, J., Pavlenko, I. (eds.) MANUFACTURING 2022. LNME, pp. 241–252. Springer, Cham (2022). https://doi.org/10.1007/978-3-030-99310-8_19

36. Unity. https://unity.com/. Accessed 04 Nov 2022

37. Unreal Engine, https://www.unrealengine.com/. Accessed 04 Nov 2022

38. Syberfeldt, A., Danielsson, O., Gustavsson, P.: Augmented reality smart glasses in the smart factory: product evaluation guidelines and review of available products. IEEE Access **5**, 9118–9130 (2017). https://doi.org/10.1109/ACCESS.2017.2703952

39. Zhou, Y., Liu, W.: Design of virtual overhaul system for condensing steam turbine based on Unity3D. In: Proceedings of the 12th International Conference on Measuring Technology and Mechatronics Automation (ICMTMA), 28– 29. február, Phuket, pp. 204–207 (2020)

40. Stylidis, K. Dagman, A., Almius, H., et al.: Perceived quality evaluation with the use of extended reality. In: Proceedings of the Design Society: International Conference on Engineering Design, 5.– 8. august, Delft, vol. 1, no. 1, pp. 1993–2002 (2019)

41. Holubek, R., Delgado Sobrino, D. R., Koštál, P., et al.: Offline programming of an ABB robot using imported CAD models in the robotstudio software environment. Appl. Mech. Mater. **693**, 62–67 (2014). https://doi.org/10.4028/www.scientific.net/AMM.693.62

42. Luo, X., Mojica Cabico, C.D.: Development and evaluation of an augmented reality learning tool for construction engineering education. In: Proceedings of the Construction Research Congress 2018: Construction Information Technology, 2. – 4. april, New Orleans, pp. 149–159 (2018). https://doi.org/10.1061/9780784481301.015

43. Kascak, J., Teliskova, M., Torok, J., et al.: Implementation of augmented reality into the training and educational process in order to support spatial perception in technical documentation. In: Proceeding of the IEEE 6th International Conference on Industrial Engineering and Applications (ICIEA), 26. – 29. april, Tokio, pp. 583–587, (2019). https://doi.org/10.1109/IEA.2019.8715120

44. Next level BIM coordination, Revizto. https://revizto.com/en/. Accessed 04 Nov 2022

45. Lau, W.: Revizto quickly turns building models into virtual reality experiences. https://www.architectmagazine.com/technology/revizto-quickly-turns-buildingmodels-into-virtual-reality-experiences. Accessed 03 Nov 2022

46. Varonis, E.M., Varonis, M.E.: Deconstructing candy crush: what instructional design can learn from game design. Int. J. Inf. Learn. Technol. **32**(3), 150–164 (2015). https://doi.org/10.1108/IJILT-09-2014-0019

47. Dimension10. https://dimension10.com/. Accessed 03 Nov 2022

48. What is Trimble SiteVision, Trimble SiteVision. https://sitevision.trimble.com/. Accessed 02 Nov 2022

Communication Through Innovative Technologies to Increase Awareness of the Company's Brand

Annamária Behúnová[1]([⊠]) [iD] and Lucia Knapčíková[2] [iD]

[1] Faculty of Mining, Ecology, Process Control and Geotechnologies, Institute of Earth Resources, Technical University of Košice, Letná 9, 042 00 Košice, Slovak Republic
annamaria.behunova@tuke.sk
[2] Faculty of Manufacturing Technologies With a Seat in Prešov, Department of Industrial Engineering and Informatics, The Technical University of Košice, Bayerova 1, 080 01 Prešov, Slovak Republic
lucia.knapcikova@tuke.sk

Abstract. A business that wants to succeed in today's rapidly changing market must realize the importance of its customers and adapt its business activities to them. The customer must feel that he is an important part of the company and that his requirements, opinions and attitudes matter. Only in this way can the company gain its consumers' favour, trust and loyalty. Innovative technologies represent the future within the company's marketing strategy, in which entrepreneurs focus not only on the needs of the company but also on the demands of the consumer and try to interact with their customers. Through information technology, which the company implements in its company, it can get closer to its customers and thereby satisfy their subjective and objective needs. The main goal of the submitted paper is to research the possibility of developing a business entity through innovative technologies, to examine and define the relationships between the past and current state of the business and the slow development of a new marketing strategy related to the implementation of information technologies in the business environment. Deciding to introduce modern information technologies into the company's strategy means improving communication with customers, adapting business activities and final services provided to consumer requirements and specifications.

Keywords: Communication · Innovative Technologies · Brand Awareness · Market Locator

1 Introduction

In recent years, there has been enormous technological progress, which consequently had to be reflected in the economy, marketing and marketing strategies. These changes occur primarily in the external marketing environment [1]. Thus, the sociocultural, economic, political-management, technological, and competitive environment is changing [2, 3].

J. L. Afonso et al. (Eds.): SESC 2022, LNICST 502, pp. 35–45, 2023.
https://doi.org/10.1007/978-3-031-33979-0_4

All these changes caused by development and progress have forced the managers of many companies to consider whether classic forms of marketing and marketing strategies are still sufficient for the competitiveness of their companies [4, 5].

With gradual development and changes, there was also the development of the economy itself, in which Kotler identified five mechanisms that drive the economy [6, 7]:

- convergence of trade unions,
- elimination and reintroduction,
- new capabilities of society and consumers,
- customization of production,
- digitization and connectivity.

Nowadays, almost every marketing strategy focuses on the customer's existing or potential needs. The customer thus becomes the most important element of the modern economy. These needs are prioritized from the beginning, and companies place more and more emphasis on these facts, basically from the production planning itself. Most of today's companies, especially the smaller ones, believe that if there are "hard times" in the company (crisis, financial uncertainty, etc.), there is a need to radically reduce costs. That's fine, as long as you don't start saving on the business's marketing. If marketing is restricted, the company leaves room for competition, which will take full advantage of this opportunity and thus dominate part of the market. During every financial or economic crisis, the customer loses reasons to buy. If the company cannot deliver these reasons to the customer, it cannot expect growth or profit [8–11].

Current technological and marketing developments also impacted the thinking of managers who were guided by these new trends when creating new marketing strategies. The most important changes in thinking include [12–14]:

- companies do not try to manufacture every part of their product and therefore enter into agreements with suppliers and subcontractors,
- companies are not divided according to production but according to customers,
- not only management but the entire company focuses on the customer,
- focus of companies on marketing (in the past, they mainly focused on financial indicators),
- companies and managers try to keep these suppliers (longer cooperation = excellent relationship and also lower costs),
- narrow area of interest (target market),
- companies are trying to expand into global markets,
- building good relations with the customer (in the long term).

Currently, we consider text advertising and the related market locator among the basic forms of communication between sellers and consumers.

1.1 Text, Picture and Video Advertising

It is a demand-oriented, and at the same time, a demand-displayed advertising campaign in search engines google.sk, google.com, google.co.uk and others. The principle of text advertising is the display of advertising texts based on searchable words or phrases. The price of individual campaigns is determined based on a pre-set monthly budget model or for a day. The payment model is Pay Per Click (PPC). The price of a click is determined based on an auction in which all competitors who target the same target group enter. By the same target group, we mean a keyword or phrase, time (days and hours of the week), location (states, counties, cities), gender, age, interest group, etc. [15–17].

Therefore, if several competitors are focusing on the same target group, then the relevance of the texting of the advertising campaign, the relevance of the landing page (for example, if I am looking for an iPhone, the landing page that refers me to already filtered phones is more relevant than the page that refers me only to the entry page – the homepage of their e-shop), the traffic of the given website. The uniqueness of the website compared to all the websites in the world and the very important price we are willing to pay for one click [15–17].

A company with a more relevant and better-processed website with more traffic, and a better quality set advertising campaign, will invest fewer funds for a better-positioned advertising campaign within the search [18].

A picture ad, available in more than 20 different dimensions, can be displayed on more than 2 million websites worldwide. The entire Internet network can capture over 98% of the global population [19].

Different pre-defined groups can display image advertising. We can also target the target group through remarketing - targeted advertising displayed to users with which we have stored cookies that we have defined in advance. For example, it can be a website visitor who was last two weeks ago on the hillside, but at the same time, it only visited a certain subpage for us [20, 21].

Another possibility of using picture advertising is to build awareness of the so-called branding, which is "subliminal" and affects potential customers.

The principle of pricing of picture campaigns works on the model payment for 1000 views - Pay Per Mille (PPM) or the price per click - Pay Per Click (PPC).

Video advertising on the Internet is becoming increasingly popular among "small players" and discovered advertising on television. The price of such campaigns is incomparably lower compared to TV advertising [22, 23].

As far as possible, we can display video and picture ads. Video advertising can be either "unconventional" 6-s or arbitrarily long ", skipping" after 5 s. The model of campaigns for skipping advertising is paid for the number of views and clicks. In the case of non-skipping advertising, it is determined based on the booked number of advertising video views [24, 25].

1.2 Market Locator

A market locator is a direct advertising message. Personal advertising is where the company informs potential customers about its existence and new products or services provided through SMS messages [26].

Among the basic advantages of this form of advertising, we recommend [26]:

- that it is personal, i.e. this advertising message will be located among private messages, which means that it will not "fight" for space with other brands, as is the case with online advertising,

- people read SMS messages, so we can conclude that the number of readings is almost the same as the number of sendings. At the same time, we do not bother the recipient in any way, as he will receive an advertisement no more than once every two weeks,
- it is an ethical form of advertising, which means it can be quickly deleted if the user is not interested in the content of the SMS message and children do not receive it (we can optimize the target group in the next campaign),
- the possibility to share a URL link to a website or discount coupons, based on which Market Locator will measure the click-through rate.

Market locator is currently the only company in Slovakia that cooperates with three operators and allows sending advertising SMS to almost all private individuals in Slovakia, except for company numbers.

SMS can be sent for 0.07 € per SMS, while choosing the gender, age, and location is possible. However, it is also possible to target user behavior, such as travelling abroad, the client's creditworthiness, the type of device and operating system, the use of mobile data, or even the client's movement during the day. It is also possible to send an SMS at a certain time of the day, on selected days, or at a time when he is at work or, conversely, at home [26].

The advertisement follows Slovak legal standards and the GDPR (General Data Protection Regulation), as most people also consent to send advertising messages when signing contracts. Since these messages are sent directly by operators and the submitter only chooses the "type" of the user or customer to whom he wants to send the message, he does not come into contact with any personal data [26–28].

2   Work Methodology

To increase brand awareness of the investigated company, two forms of campaigns were used - image and video advertising, where the company's new logo was presented, as well as the most modern procedures and technologies available to the company [29, 30].

Specifically, the video campaign was implemented through the YouTube social network from December 2016 to February 2017. In the monitored period, the campaign's viewership reached 517,000 views, and up to 134,000 views were longer than 5 s (Fig. 1), representing 25.90% of total views. The average cost per view was €0.02/view of 1 video.

In a more detailed analysis of video views longer than 5 s, based on audience retention statistics, it was shown that less than 40% of site visitors watched 25% of the total video length, almost 30% of the audience watched 50% of the total video length, and 20% of visitors website watched the entire video (Fig. 2), which represents 26,800 views in three months.

Regarding the demographic indicators - gender and age- we also observed when analyzing the advertising campaign and the number of clicks on it. When analyzing the number of views, we concluded that, in this case, the video campaign was seen equally by men and women. The difference was only in the age composition of the followers, where the largest group consisted of men in the age group of 35–44 years and women in the age group of 25–34 years (Fig. 3).

The research was carried out on a sample where up to 71% of the respondents' gender and age were known.

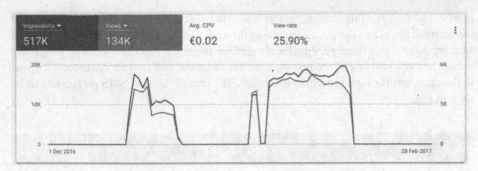

Fig. 1. Number of video views in the period December 2016 - February 2017 [Authors own processing]

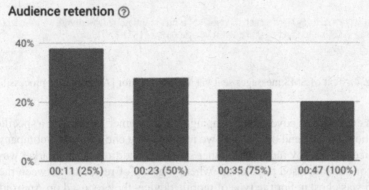

Fig. 2. Follower retention rate [Authors own processing]

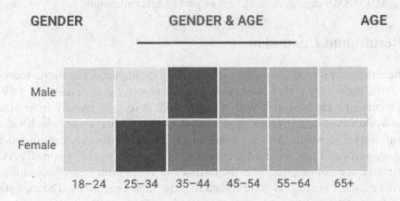

Based on the 71% of your video views with known gender and age. ⑦

Fig. 3. Age group and gender of followers [Authors own processing]

To increase awareness of the brand, online interviews with the head of the clinic were also carried out, and a flyer campaign was supplemented with a PR article. Still, the latest marketing strategy of the company, which sought to increase awareness of the brand - of the company, was an advertising campaign through Market Locator, which took place in January 2019. The campaign's goal was to inform the target market - potential customers about the possibility of a free professional examination and thus increase their interest in the company through sent SMS messages. The text of the sent SMS messages can be seen in Fig. 4.

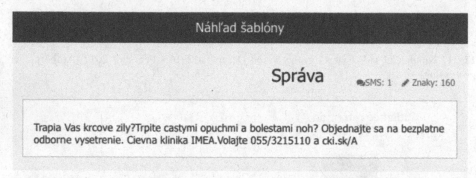

Fig. 4. Text of SMS messages sent via Market Locator [Authors own processing]

When creating this advertising campaign, the customer can choose a specific market to which he wants to send messages. Two regions were chosen for the company's needs - the Košice and Prešov regions. Another specific condition of the market was the age structure of the addressed population, where a group of residents between the ages of 35 and 65 was chosen. For the type of mobile device, they focused on Android, iPhone and Blackberry and for the use of mobile data of more than 100 MB (Fig. 5). A total of over 200,000 SMS messages were sent as part of this campaign.

3   Results and Discussion

For the most accurate and up-to-date comparison of the impact of innovative technologies on website traffic, the period January-April 2020 (users, blue curves) and 2019 (users, orange curves) were analyzed. Within this period, at its end, namely from March, the whole world was affected by the Coronavirus (COVID-19) pandemic, which had and still hurts all market segments. As it is a pandemic, the kind of humanity has not experienced for many years and was not even prepared for, the whole world "stopped". As part of the declared state of emergency in the territory of the Slovak Republic and the related restrictions, most businesses were forced to close their operations. The exception was hospitals, pharmacies, drugstores, and food and gas stations. The investigated company was closed during this period, and promotional events and all company activities were limited. This was also reflected in the research results and even more pointed out the power of the influence of innovative technologies and marketing of the company.

The website traffic curves clearly show this situation in Fig. 6, where we can see how the site's traffic dropped rapidly from March to April 2020. For comparison - in March 2019, the site's traffic reached the highest values, while in March 2020 reached

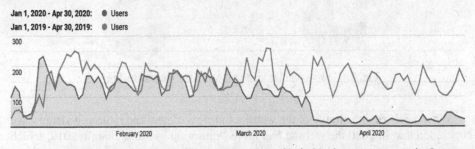

Podmienka #1

Vek - Základná Socio-Demografická SK

☑ Označiť / odznačiť všetko ☐ Nedostupné ☐ Pod 18 ☐ 18 - 26 ☐ 26 - 35

☑ 35 - 45 ☑ 45 - 55 ☑ 55 - 65 ☐ Nad 65

Okres, kraj - Spacia lokalita - Typická lokalita

< ☐ Slovenská republika

Typ mobilného telefónu - Využívanie mobilu

☑ Označiť / odznačiť všetko ☑ Nedostupné ☐ Klasický bez OS ☑ Android ☑ iPhone

☑ Blackberry ☐ Symbian ☐ Windows ☐ MacOS

Pohlavie - Základná Socio-Demografická SK

☑ Označiť / odznačiť všetko ☐ Nedostupné ☑ Ženy ☑ Muži

Využívanie mobilných dát - Využívanie mobilu

☑ Označiť / odznačiť všetko ← 💬 🗑 → 100 MB ☑ 100 MB - 1 GB
☑ 1 GB

Fig. 5. Specification of target market conditions [Authors own processing]

only half the traffic, and in the second half of the month, it fell to the lowest values of the analyzed periods. April 2020 continuously reached very low traffic values. On average, there were only 20 visits per day, which compared to April 2019, where the average daily visits were at the level of 180-page visits per day, represents a decrease in website traffic by 89%.

Jan 1, 2020 - Apr 30, 2020: ● Users
Jan 1, 2019 - Apr 30, 2019: ● Users

300

200

100

February 2020   March 2020   April 2020

Fig. 6. Website traffic during the COVID-19 pandemic [Authors own processing]

A more detailed treatment of the decline in website traffic according to several monitored indicators can be seen in Table 1. When comparing traffic-site users for 2019 and 2020, there was a decrease of up to 5,772 users, representing a decrease of up to 37.93% compared to 2019. When analyzing new users and visitors to the site, there was a decrease of 5,700 users, representing a decrease of up to 38.98%.

Table 1. Website traffic indicators

Pointer	2019	2020	% change
User	15,217	9,445	−37.93%
New user	14,624	8,924	−38.98%
Sessions	23,926	14,199	−40.65%
Number of sessions per user	1,570	1,500	−4.39%
View page	52,429	30,120	−42.55%
Site / Session	2,190	2,120	−3.20%
Average session duration	3:45 min	3:16 min	−12.96%
Bounce rate	15.67%	16.92%	7.96%

This situation had the biggest impact on meeting metrics and page views. In meetings, we can note a decrease of 9,727 users, i.e. up to 40.65%. Page views, which achieved the largest decrease for the analyzed period up to 42.55%, are 22,309 fewer page views in 2020 than 2019.On the contrary, the average session duration indicator is a positive factor, based on a decrease of 12.96%, representing only 29 s for the average duration of a one-page view. Despite the pandemic and slight declines in some of the analyzed areas of website traffic, based on a comprehensive summary analysis of the number of visits to the company's website for the period 2016–2020, we can conclude that website traffic has an upward trend, which can be seen in Fig. 7.

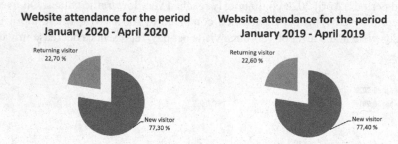

Fig. 7. New vs regular visitors [Authors own processing]

When analyzing the traffic of the website in terms of new and returning visitors, we concluded that in 2020 the website had more "returning" visitors than in 2019, which means that despite the bad impact of the crisis on all business spheres, the company managed to keep its regular customers. We can consider this as a very positive factor in the evaluation of brand building and customer relations, that despite the difficult situation that occurred in the market, the company managed to increase the ratio of regular visitors compared to 2019 (Fig. 8).

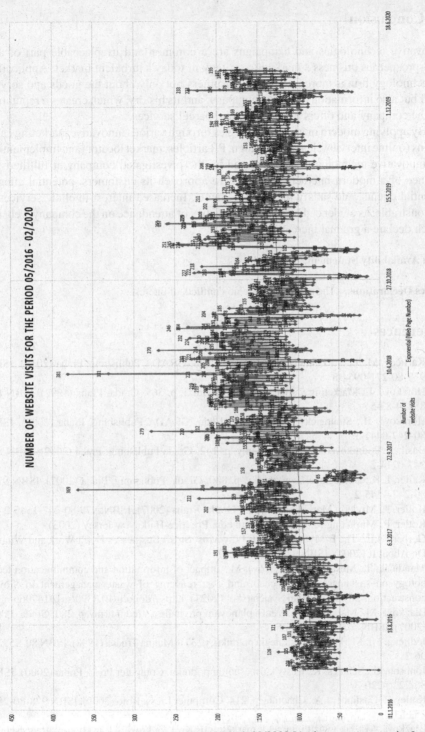

Fig. 8. Number of visits for the period 05/2016–02/2020 [Authors own processing]

4 Conclusion

Innovative technologies and campaigns are a common and irreplaceable part of any well-prosperous business's marketing strategy in today's turbulent market. Application of technology brings more interest to consumers not only about the goods and service itself but also information about the company, and its history, which creates a reputation for the company and offers of shopping and parcel services.

By applying modern marketing strategies through various innovative marketing campaigns (online interview, leaflet campaign, PR articles, market locator) and implementing the innovative technologies implemented by the investigated company, it fulfilled the essence of a modern interactive business to approach its customers, potential clients, potential clients, and satisfy their requirements. Increased interest in clinic services is demonstrable, as evidenced by outputs - statistics of attendance on the company website, which declare a gradual increase in traffic.

Data Availability Statement.   Not applicable.

Ethics Declarations.   The authors declare no conflicts of interest.

References

1. Karlíček, M., et al.: Základy marketingu, p. 288. GRADA Publishing, Praha (2018). ISBN 978-80-271-0954-8
2. Horáková, I.: Marketing v současné světové praxi, p. 365. Grada, Praha (1992). ISBN 80-85424-83-5
3. Horáková, H.: Strategický Marketing. 2nd edn. GRADA Publishing, Praha (2003). ISBN 80-247-0447-1
4. Basil, J.: Podnikovéinformační systémy, p. 142. Grada Publishing, Praha (2002). ISBN 80-247-0214-2
5. Keller, L.K.: Strategickéřízení značky, p. 800. Grada, Publishing, Praha (2007). ISBN 978-80-247-1545-2
6. Kotler, P.: Moderní Marketing, p. 1048. Grada, Praha (2007). ISBN: 978-80-247-1545-2
7. Kotler, P.: Marketing Management, 11th edn. Prentice-Hall, New Jersey (2003)
8. Gerber, M.E.: The E-Myth Revisited: Why Most Small Businesses Don't Work and What to Do About It (2004). ISBN 978-0887307287
9. Mandičák, T., Mésároš, P., Spišáková, M.: Impact of information and communication technology on sustainable supply chain and cost reducing of waste management in Slovak construction. Sustain. Bazilej Švajčiarsko. (2021). https://doi.org/10.3390/su13147966
10. Blažková, M.: Marketingové řízení a plánovaní pro mále a střední firmy, p. 280. Grada, Praha (2007). ISBN 978-80-247-1535-3
11. Jedlička, M.: Marketingová stratégia podniku, p. 371. Magna Trnava (1998). ISBN 80-85722-06-2
12. Johnson, G., Scholes, K.: Cesty k úspěšnému podniku. Computer Press, Praha (2000). ISBN 80-7226-220-3
13. Kotler, P., Caslione, J.A.: Chaotika, p. 214. Computer Press, Brno (2009). ISBN 978-80-251-2599-1
14. Blažková, M.: Jak využít internet v marketingu: Krok za krokem k vyšší konkurenceschopnosti. 1. vyd., p. 156. Grada Publishing, Praha (2005). ISBN 80-247-1095-1

15. Blecker, T.: Information and Management Systems for Product Customization, p. 266. Springer, New York (2005). ISBN 0-387-23347-4, https://doi.org/10.1007/b101300
16. Google Marketingováplatforma. https://analytics.google.com/analytics/web/provision/#/provision. Accessed 10 Oct 2022
17. Hesková, M., Štarchoň, P.: Marketingová komunikace a moderní trendy v marketingu, p. 180. Oeconomica, Praha (2009). ISBN 9788024515205
18. Burns, T., Stalker, G.M.: The Management of Innovation. Tavistock Publications, London (1961). ISBN 0-198-28878-6
19. Dodson, I.: The Art of Digital Marketing. Wiley, Hoboken (2016). ISBN 978-1119265702
20. Didner, P.: Global Content Marketing: How to Create Great Content, Reach More Customers, and Build a Worldwide Marketing Strategy that Works (2014). ISBN 978-0071840972
21. Dietrisch, G.: Spin Sucks: Communication and Reputation Management in the Digital Age (Que Biz-Tech) (2014). ISBN 978-0789748867
22. Kingsnorth, S.: Digital Marketing Strategy: An Integrated Approach to Online Marketing, 1st edn (2016). ISBN 978-0749474706
23. Karlíček, M., Král, P.: Marketingová komunikace: Jak komunikovat na našem trhu. 1st edn. Grada Publishing, Praha (2011). ISBN 978-80-247-3541-2
24. Fox, V.: Marketing vevěku společnosti Google (2011). ISBN 978-80-251-3357-6
25. Kauffman, S.A.: The Origins of Order: Self-Organization and Selection in Evolution. Oxford University Press, New York (1993). ISBN 0-195-07951-5
26. Marketlocator – Esemeska dostane Vašu reklamu do vrecka 1,8 milióna Slovákov, https://www.marketlocator.sk/. Accessed 10 Oct 2022
27. Periša, M., Cvitić, I., Peraković, D., Husnjak, S.: Beacon technology for real-time informing the traffic network users about the environment. Transport **34**, 373–382 (2019). https://doi.org/10.3846/transport.2019.10402
28. Matulić, I., Msa, M., Peraković, D.: Information and communication infrastructure for the organisation of railway passenger transport. In: Čokorilo, O. (ed.) Proceedings of the Second International Conference on Traffic and Transport Engineering ICTTE. City Net Scientific Research Center Ltd. Belgrade, Belgrade, Serbia, pp. 410–419 (2014)
29. Straka, M., Khouri, S., Rosova, A., Caganova, D., Čulkova, K.: Utilization of computer simulation for waste separation design as a logistics system. Int. J. Simul. Model. Rakúsko **17**(4), 583–596 (2018). https://doi.org/10.2507/IJSIMM17(4)444
30. Periša, M., Kuljanić, T.M., Cvitić, I., Kolarovszki, P.: Conceptual model for informing user with innovative smart wearable device in industry 4.0. Wirel. Netw. **27**(3), 1615–1626 (2019). https://doi.org/10.1007/s11276-019-02057-9

Advancement of Circular Economy Supported by Intelligent Communication System

Annamária Behúnová[1] (iD), Lucia Knapčíková[2]([⊠]) (iD), and Matúš Martiček[2]

[1] Faculty of Mining, Ecology, Process Control and Geotechnologies, Institute of Earth Resources, Technical University of Košice, Prešov, Slovak Republic
annamaria.behunova@tuke.sk
[2] Faculty of Manufacturing Technologies With a Seat in Prešov, Department of Industrial Engineering and Informatics, The Technical University of Košice, Bayerova 1, 080 01 Prešov, Slovak Republic
lucia.knapcikova@tuke.sk, matus.marticek@student.tuke.sk

Abstract. However, the linear economy and its current model will not be able to ensure long-term sustainability. It is not appropriate, and above all possible, to increase production from primary sources indefinitely. In some areas, it directly affects the population's life. It brings negative elements, such as climate change, increasing differences between poor and rich regions, and natural disasters with more serious consequences. Emerging problems such as the deterioration of air, soil and water quality directly impact declining human well-being. But there is an economic model in which such non-ecological behaviour and waste of resources do not occur. This model is called a circular economy. The manuscript is focused on applying the circular economy within the enterprises of the Slovak Republic and individual EU states. An important task will be to use the information system and the method for obtaining data and subsequent processing. A properly set up circular economy can minimize the waste of resources, improve the efficiency of their use, reduce g reenhouse gas emissions and contribute to the preservation of biodiversity.

Keywords: Monitoring · Communication · Circular Economy · Sustainability

1 Introduction

Circular economy (CE), also called circular economy, is an economic model whose main goal is to reuse resources [1]. It is about changing the point of view of consumed goods. We no longer consider them as waste. We consider them as possible inputs. An important role is played by adopting sophisticated solutions that can bring new value to consumed goods and thus re-enter the economic process [2]. The circular economy changes the concept of "take-throw-away", which is characteristic of the linear economy, to the idea of cyclicity in (circulation), from which the name "circular (circular) economy" comes. [3, 4] Regarding energy, the circular economy prefers renewable resources naturally present in our biospheres, such as solar energy, water or wind current. It aims to minimize

J. L. Afonso et al. (Eds.): SESC 2022, LNICST 502, pp. 46–55, 2023.
https://doi.org/10.1007/978-3-031-33979-0_5

or even eliminate the use of toxic chemicals that harm the environment and represent a barrier to their reprocessing. [5, 6] The main task of the corporate information system is processing data that is created in the organization. Therefore, data processing can only be considered one of the subsystems of the information system. The information system consists of people, and technical and program resources to ensure the collection, transmission, processing, distribution, storage, selection and presentation of information for the needs of managers so that they can perform their management functions in all management system components (Fig. 1).

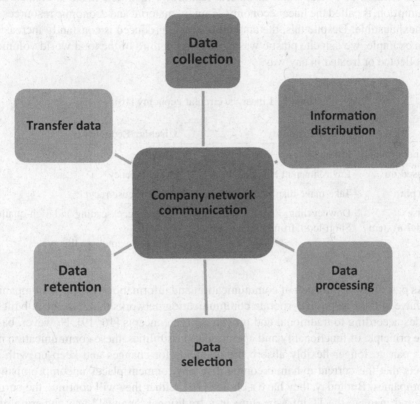

Fig. 1. Company network communication process [Authors own processing]

A very important part of the information system is the automated information system, which is ensured through computer technology. When applying the circular economy in the company, collecting, gathering and processing data is an important task [7, 8]. The main goal of the information system is also to achieve the highest possible quality in the shortest possible time and at the lowest possible cost [4, 18]. Currently, the information system significantly affects real human knowledge in various spheres. An individual needs new information for his management method and decision-making, which must be provided to him constantly, in the necessary quantity and quality. A comparison of the basic factors of the linear and circular economy is in Tab. 1. Today's society is characterized by high consumption [3, 13]. That is, we have been living for a long time in a way where we extract many natural resources, which we then transport to the opposite end of the world. There, it is processed using expensive technologies, the products are manufactured, and then they have transported again to other countries of the world, where consumers can purchase and consume them [5, 23]. After consumption, consumers throw away used, consumed products or just their remains, which creates waste that ends up many times thrown in the wild or the best case, ends up in incinerators or landfills. We can rightly consider this method of consumption as devastating and unsustainable socially, economically and environmentally [4, 9].

The method of consumption of natural resources, in which waste is created after consumption, is called the linear economy. Human, material and economic resources are not inexhaustible. Despite this, the amount of waste produced is constantly increasing. As an example, we can cite plastic waste, of which a third of the total world volume is not collected or treated in any way.

Table 1. Linear vs. circular economy [10].

	Linear Economy	Circular Economy
Business model	Product	Services
Focused on	Environmental efficiency	Eco-efficiency
Step plan	Take-make-dispose	Reduce-reuse-recycle
Re-use Border system	Downcycling Short-term, from purchase to sale	Upcycling, cascading and high-quality recycling Long-term, multiple life cycles

As part of the application of communication and information systems in companies, they have at their disposal corporate communication networks that have been built for decades according to traditional and proven design concepts [16, 19]. However, based on the principle of functionality and operational possibilities, these communication networks can no longer flexibly absorb the demands for changes and keep up with the markets that the current dynamic competitive environment places uncompromisingly on companies. But today, they have a choice [10]. Either they will continue the current trend and manage the IT infrastructure in a traditional "manual" way, where almost every change in communication parameters means implementing a larger or smaller IT project [11]. However, such a time-consuming activity can also threaten the company to gradually retreat from its position in today's dynamic competitive environment. Or they fundamentally change the design of the IT infrastructure and, with it, their idea of how to operate it, and implement technical solutions based on so-called software-defined networks, which are based on the total automation of activities connected with the operation of corporate communication networks [12, 18].

1.1 Circular Economy Supported by Company Network Communication System

After defining its long-term and short-term goals and their subsequent achievement, the company implements many activities. In the mutual interaction of business activities, the inputs necessary for realizing business performance turn into outputs - this process is called the transformation process. We can define it as a set of business activities to change business inputs into results. This process cannot be perceived in isolation, only in close ties to other systems [13]. The transformation process (Fig. 1) is one of the basic features of the company's functioning when inputs are transformed into outputs (products, goods, and services) through the transformation process. The goal is to maximize profit, and its hallmark is economy. In connection with the complex transformation system, inputs are provided by the supplier system and outputs by the customer (user) system [13, 15] (Fig. 2).

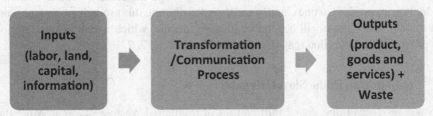

Fig. 2. Transformation and communication process of circular economy [Authors own processing].

2 Work Methodology

For the circular economy to enter the thinking and behavior of producers and consumers, as it is a new innovative and in many cases, unknown approach, it is necessary to understand it. The main principles of the circular economy form the basis of this theory [14, 19]:

- For a customer, a consumer, his status as a consumer changes to the status of a user. With CE, companies will want back materials from products when the product has lost its value from the customer's point of view. This approach by manufacturers could intensive customers to return items at the end of their useful life [14, 17, 31].
- CE aims to produce zero waste. A minimum of waste is thrown away because the waste can be further used in various ways. For example, by re-using what should not have been used in the linear economy. Or by fixing what is broken and remaking what can no longer be improved. This principle works based on not adding any primary raw materials to the process but working with those raw materials that have already been used at least once [15, 18].
- For this industrial production cycle to be truly sustainable, the energy that enters it and drives it should also be almost completely renewable. The use of renewable energy would also lead to a reduction in the risk of resource depletion for businesses or fluctuations in energy supply. In the absolute sense, this would also reduce part of the costs for the actual production of the products [17, 27]

- According to the fourth principle, there are two types of industrial additives to products. They can be disposable (they can biodegrade in nature, for example, paper or fabric) or durable ("technical", for example, metal, glass or plastic, which can be reused relatively easily). The products should belong to one or the other group so that everything can then be reused or returned to nature, where the ingredients used in the product will naturally decompose. The design of more complex objects should be designed in such a way that the objects can be disassembled and subsequently so that they can be classified into these two categories at the end of the life of a certain product and further used properly according to this division [16, 18].

The main goal of the circular economy is to change the current popular system of producing one product in one country and then distributing this product around the world to a system where there will be smaller local producers, which would bring more jobs and prosperity to areas that may not have had it before [17, 23].

2.1 Circular Map in the Slovak Republic

Slovakia produces more than 2 million tons of municipal waste every year. More than half of it ends up in landfills. We use natural resources, often non-renewable, to create new products while our consumption grows exponentially [17, 19]. We throw away thousands of products every day, wasting the resources that were used to make them. The Slovak Republic is set to the so-called linear economy in which we take natural resources - create a product - depreciate through use - and throw them away. Even from this simplified view, it is obvious that such a principle cannot work in the long term. Reuse and sharing, repairability, upcycling, and, in the final phase, striving for zero waste are the basic pillars of the circular economy [18, 19]. The transition to an efficient circular economy at the level of individuals, producers, and municipalities is facilitated by several tools resulting from experts from various organizations (Fig. 3).

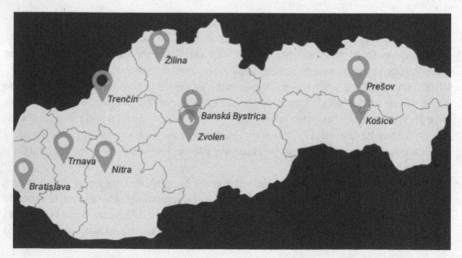

Fig. 3. The circular map of the Slovak Republic [21].

The circular economy tries to create services and places that help us prevent waste: reuse centers, repair shops, libraries, community composting sites, rental shops, packaging-free shops. And precisely, circular maps contain lists of these places important for the circular economy (circular economy), the goal of which is not to create waste, but on the contrary, to use it as a source of material or energy [20, 24]. This map is a guide on how to handle waste more responsibly. The map is intended to help all state residents and visitors to individual cities find ways to prevent waste and use the services of the sharing economy [21]. Municipalities and towns thus always have an up-to-date overview of data available 24/7.

3 Results and Discussion

Recycled waste represents processed waste that has been sent to other forms of recovery than energy recovery. Wastewater data are adjusted for waste collected in one state and recycled in another [20, 23]. The waste-recycling indicator expresses the ratio of recycled waste to the total processed waste, multiplied by 100, as this indicator is expressed in %. Both of these indicators are measured in tons. This indicator applies to hazardous and non-hazardous waste from all economic sectors and households, including waste from waste processing (secondary waste), except for mineral waste. [21, 23]. Mineral waste is excluded in order to avoid situations where trends in the production of ordinary waste can be "drowned" due to massive fluctuations in the production of waste in the mining and mineral transformation industry. It also allows for a more meaningful comparison between countries, as mineral waste represents significant amounts in countries characterized mainly by the mining and construction sectors. [20] The change in the rate of wastewater recycling in the period from 2010 to 2018 is shown graphically in Fig. 3. The higher the value - the percentage of the waste recycling rate, the more waste is secondary processed, and the less waste ends up in landfills, incinerators or just thrown away, often in the wild [21, 22].

Based on the analysis, we can conclude that in 2010 there were only nine states within the European Union (out of a total of 28 countries) whose waste recycling rate was higher than the European average (53%). In 2014 it was already in 11 countries (which had a higher percentage of recycling than the European average of 55%), and in 2018 it was also in 11 countries, but this year the European average was 56% [22] (Fig. 4).

One of the indicators of the application of the circular economy to the economy of a given country is the rate of use of circular material (CM) [22]. This indicator measures the share of recycled material and its reuse in the economy, which leads to a reduction in the amount of extracted primary raw materials in the overall use of the material. Circulating material usage, also known as circulation rate, is defined as the ratio of circulating material used to total material used [23, 27]. The total use of the material is equal to the sum of the total domestic consumption of material and the use of circulating material. Using recycled material approaches the amount of waste recycled in domestic waste recovery facilities minus imported manure intended for recovery plus exported waste intended for recovery abroad [24]. Waste recycled in domestic waste recovery facilities includes recovery activities, defined in the Waste framework directive

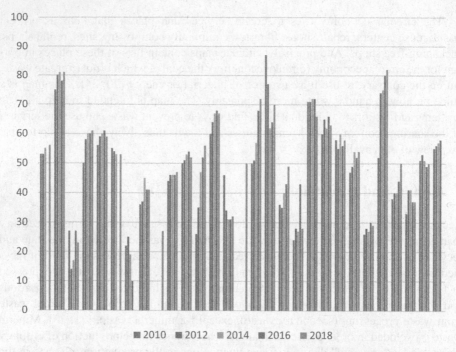

Fig. 4. Recycling rate in EU countries in the period 2010–2018 [22].

75/442/EEC. [21] The rate of use of circulating material has changed over the years in individual countries of the European Union (Fig. 5) It declares the change in the rate of use of circulating material in the period 2010–2020 and a graphic representation of the map of Europe in the period 2010–2020 [22, 25].

The higher the value of the recycling material utilization rate, the more secondary materials replace primary raw materials, which reduces the environmental impact of primary material extraction [26, 29]. Unlike the linear one, the circular economy works in closed circles: biological and technical. Within those circles, materials move, and there is no waste, because the circular economy perceives waste as a resource [27, 29]. Because he is: textiles as a source for building material, food waste as a source for the paper industry, bio-waste as a source for agriculture. This systemic change is not a choice for people, but an obligation. It requires the cooperation of all areas of society, from consumers, designers and material experts, developers, companies, and investors, to the third sector, academics and politicians [28].

However, unless countries around the world implement the "polluter pays" rule and economically favour ecological business (for example, by taxing carbon dioxide production), the transition of companies and their customers to green mode will be more or less only a matter of personal conviction [19, 28].

Although the current economic system knows the concept of renting, long-term borrowing is perceived as economically disadvantageous. In the circular economy, renting is the basis for completely new business models in all sectors of life, which fundamentally

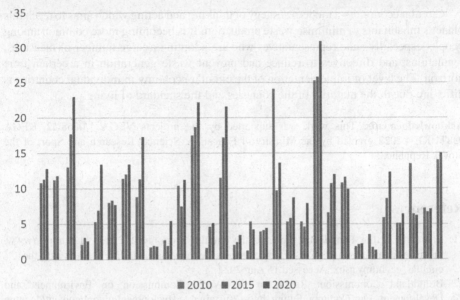

Fig. 5. Transformation and communication process of circular economy [22].

change how products are owned [29, 31]. Consumers become users who buy the service, that is, the flawless functioning and performance of the products, not the product itself.

Companies are the owners of the products and are also responsible for their maintenance, repairs, energy efficiency and recovery. Such a system is a win-win for everyone. Users do not have to worry about repairs or high one-time purchase costs, allowing many to have a better standard of living and use first-class products [30].

Companies are motivated to produce quality products and design them so they can be evaluated as best as possible. Waste, dependence on raw materials and negative impacts on the environment or human health are eliminated. A fundamental part of this effort is a change in the approach to product design.

Another key element in building a circular economy is creating new business models and reforming existing supply chains [31]. By moving from transactional models to contractual models (i.e. models where products are seen as a service), companies can work more closely with their customers and contribute to a strategy that keeps products out of the landfill [32].

4 Conclusion

Innovations in the field of production and processing of mineral raw materials through the transformation process always bring with them new possibilities, which on the one hand, are positive. There is a faster, more efficient, more variable transformation of inputs into outputs. Still, on the other hand, such rapid and uncontrolled consumption greatly burdens nature and the environment. It is, therefore, necessary to stop, or at least slowdown, this fast consumer lifestyle and think about your actions.

Circular economy - a modern strategy of thinking and acting which aims to teach this planet's inhabitants to minimise waste production. It is becoming more common among people, especially state representatives who are adopting a large number of measures, regulations, and directives to reduce and prevent waste generation in a certain time horizon. The level of implementation of the circular economy in individual countries is different, due to the maturity of the countries and the standard of living.

Acknowledgements. This work was supported by the projects VEGA 1/0268/22, KEGA 038TUKE-4/2022 granted by the Ministry of Education, Science, Research and Sport of the Slovak Republic.

References

1. Ellen MacArthur Foundation: Towards the circular economy 2. 2013. 112. https://www.mckinsey.com/~/media/mckinsey/dotcom/client_service/sustainability/pdfs/towards_the_circular_economy.ashx. Accessed 15 Aug 2022
2. Brundtland Commission: Report of the World Commission on Environment and Development- Our Common Future. https://sustainabledevelopment.un.org/content/documents/5987our-common-future.pdf. Accessed 25 Jul 2022
3. Periša, M., Cvitić, I., Peraković, D., Husnjak, S.: Beacon technology for real-time informing the traffic network users about the environment. Transport **34**, 373–382 (2019). https://doi.org/10.3846/transport.2019.10402
4. Matulić, I., Msa, M., Peraković, D.: Information and communication infrastructure for the organisation of railway passenger transport. In: Čokorilo, O. (ed.) Proceedings of the Second International Conference on Traffic and Transport Engineering ICTTE. City Net Scientific Research Center Ltd. Belgrade, Belgrade, Serbia, pp. 410–419 (2014)
5. Peña Miñano, S., et al.: A review of digital wayfinding technologies in the transportation industry. In: Advances in Transdisciplinary Engineering. IOS Press BV, pp. 207–212 (2017)
6. Nagyova, A., Pacaiova, H., Markulik, S., et al.: Design of a model for risk reduction in project management in small and medium-sized enterprises. Symetry-Basel **13**(5) (2021). https://doi.org/10.3390/sym13050763
7. Straka, M., Khouri, S., et al.: Utilization of computer simulation for waste separation design as a logistics system. Int. J. Simul. Model. **17**(4), 83–596 (2018). https://doi.org/10.2507/IJSIMM17(4)444
8. Pacaiova, H., Sinay, J., Markulik, S., et al.: Measuring the qualitative actors on copper wire surface. Measurement **109**, 359–365 (2017). https://doi.org/10.1016/j.measurement.2017.06.002
9. European Commission: Investing in a climate-neutral and circular economy. Available on https://ec.europa.eu/commission/presscorner/detail/en/fs_20_40/. Accessed 21 Apr 2022
10. Bonciu, F.: The European economy: from a linear to a circular economy. Romanian J. Eur. affairs, **14**(4) (2014). ISSN: 1582-8271
11. Periša, M., Kuljanić, T.M., Cvitić, I., Kolarovszki, P.: Conceptual model for informing user with innovative smart wearable device in industry 4.0. Wireless Netw. **27**(3), 1615–1626 (2019). https://doi.org/10.1007/s11276-019-02057-9
12. Meinig, M., Sukmana, M.I., Torkura, K.A., Meinel, C.J.P.C.S.: Holistic strategy-based threat model for organizations. Proc. Comput. Sci. **151**, 100–107 (2019)
13. Islam, M.A., Vrbsky, S.V.: Transaction management with tree-based consistency in cloud databases. Int. J. Cloud Comput. **6**(1), 58–78 (2017)

14. Kirchherr, J., et al.: Barriers to the circular economy - evidence from the European Union (EU). Ecol. Econ. **150**, 264–272 (2018). ISSN: 0921-8009 56

15. Gou, Z., Yamaguchi, S., e al.: Analysis of various security issues and challenges in cloud computing environment: a survey. In: Identity Theft: Breakthroughs in Research and Practice, pp. 221–247. IGI global (2017)

16. Olakanmi, O.O., Dada, A.: An efficient privacy-preserving approach for secure verifiable outsourced computing on untrusted platforms. Int. J. Cloud Appl. Comput. (IJCAC) **9**(2), 79–98 (2019)

17. Prandi, C., Nunes, N., Ribeiro, M., Nisi, V.: Enhancing sustainable mobility awareness by exploiting multi-sourced data: The case study of the Madeira Islands. Sustainable Internet and ICT for Sustainability (SustainIT), Funchal, pp. 1–5 (2017)

18. Hugos, M.H., Hulitzky, D.: Business in the Cloud: What Every Business needs To Know About Cloud Computing, p. 139. John Wiley & Sons (2010)

19. Lee, C.K.M., Zhang, S.Z., Ng, K.K.H.: Development of an industrial Internet of things suite for smart factory towards re-industrialization. Adv. Manuf. **5**(4), 335–343 (2017). https://doi.org/10.1007/s40436-017-0197-2

20. Ungurean, I., Gaitan, N.-C., Gaitan, V.: A middleware based architecture for the industrial internet of things. 10.28742891 (2016).https://doi.org/10.3837/tiis.2016.07.001

21. Circular map. https://nasebio-eko.sk/cirkularna-mapa-slovensko/. Accessed 16 Nov 2022

22. Globa, L., Kurdecha, V., Ishchenko,I., Zakharchuk, A., Kunieva, N.: The Intellectual IoT-system for monitoring the base station quality of service. In: 2018 IEEE International Black Sea Conference on Communications and Networking (BlackSeaCom), Batumi, pp. 1–5 (2018). https://doi.org/10.1109/BlackSeaCom.2018.8433715

23. Babaria, U.: IoT development needs microservices and containerization (2018). https://www.einfochips.com/blog/why-iot-development-needs-microservices-and-containerization

24. Mijling, B., Jiang, Q., de Jonge, D., Bocconi, S.: Field calibration of electrochemical NO_2 sensors in a citizen science context. Atmos. Meas. Tech. **11**, 1297–1312 (2018). https://doi.org/10.5194/amt-11-1297-2018

25. Spinelle, L., Gerboles, M., Aleixandre, M.: Performance evaluation of amperomet-ric sensors for the monitoring of O_3 and NO_2 in ambient air at PPB level. Procedia Eng. **120**, 480–483 (2015). https://doi.org/10.1016/j.pro-eng.2015.08.676

26. Catini, A., et al.: Development of a sensor node for remote monitoring of plants. Sensors. **19**, 4865 (2019)

27. Christakis, I., Hloupis, G., Stavrakas, I., Tsakiridis, O.: Low cost sensor implemen-tation and evaluation for measuring NO2 and O3 pollutants. In: 2020 9th Interna-tional Conference on Modern Circuits and Systems Technologies (MOCAST), pp. 1–4. IEEE (2020)

28. Tryner, J., et al.: Laboratory evaluation of low-cost PurpleAir PM monitors and in-field correction using co-located portable filter samplers. Atmospheric Environ. **220**, 117067 (2020)

29. Giordano, M.R., et al.: From low-cost sensors to high-quality data: a summary of challenges and best practices for effectively calibrating low-cost par-ticulate matter mass sensors. J. Aerosol Sci. **158**, 105833 (2021). https://doi.org/10.1016/j.jaerosci.2021.105833

30. Rai, A.C., et al.: End-user perspective of low-cost sensors for outdoor air pollution monitoring. Sci. Total Environ. **607–608**, 691–705 (2017). https://doi.org/10.1016/j.scitotenv.2017.06.266

31. Goldemberg, J., Martinez-Gomez, J., Sagar, A., Smith, K.R.: Household air pollution, health, and climate change: cleaning the air. Environ. Res. Lett. **13**, 030201 (2018). https://doi.org/10.1088/1748-9326/aaa49d

32. Malings, C., et al.: Development of a general calibration model and long-term performance evaluation of low-cost sensors for air pollutant gas monitor-ing. Atmos. Meas. Tech. **12**, 903–920 (2019). https://doi.org/10.5194/amt-12-903-2019

Techno-economic Assessment of Traffic-Adaptive Smart Lighting Projects

Tebello N. D. Mathaba(✉)

Postgraduate School of Engineering Management, University of Johannesburg, Johannesburg, South Africa
tmathaba@uj.ac.za

Abstract. Rapid population growth in cities results in an increased energy consumption and need for infrastructure development. Street lights are some of the common energy consuming infrastructure in cities. Energy efficiency and demand-side management (EEDSM) interventions are therefore required to lower emissions and energy intensity in cities as well as save costs. The upgrading of infrastructure to include internet-of-things technologies as cities transition towards 'smart cities' presents opportunities to save energy via retrofitting old street light technology with smart lights. This work presents a methodology for techno-economic analysis of evaluating smart lighting retrofit projects that use traffic-adaptive control. The proposed analysis uses a lamp failure rate model to conduct a techno-economic analysis of street lights in a case-study city in South Africa. The resulting payback period for the smart lights retrofit is 3.42 years. The methodology proposed in this paper is more comprehensive than current alternatives in literature; it incorporates the time-value of money, makes use of lighting simulation studies and offers more accurate calculations of maintenance costs.

Keywords: Smart city · Energy efficiency · Streetlights · Smart light

1 Introduction

The population in cities is increasing rapidly, with African cities growing at an annual rate of 3.5% and half of the African population is expected to live in cities by 2030 [1]. This phenomenon is expected to increase energy consumption in cities. The energy use in cities is projected to reach 73% of global energy consumption by 2030. Cities are major sources of carbon emissions, for example accounting for as high as 85% of the national total in China [2]. Thus, there is a need to have energy efficiency interventions to contribute towards the United

© ICST Institute for Computer Sciences, Social Informatics and Telecommunications Engineering 2023
Published by Springer Nature Switzerland AG 2023. All Rights Reserved
J. L. Afonso et al. (Eds.): SESC 2022, LNICST 502, pp. 56–66, 2023.
https://doi.org/10.1007/978-3-031-33979-0_6

Nation's sustainable development goal (SGD) number 11 - *"Make cities and human settlements inclusive, safe, resilient and sustainable"*.

Lighting in cities is expected to account for about 19% of energy consumption, where a significant portion will be dedicated to street lighting [3]. The light emitting diode (LED) lighting technology is the predominantly recommended alternative for retrofitting the older technologies like the fluorescent, mercury vapour (MV) [4], high pressure sodium (HPS) [5] and metal-halide [6].

LED technology is attractive due to its high luminous efficacy. For example, it is shown to be 1.8× more than that of HPS at 150 W in [5]. Thus, many projects advocate for the retrofitting of current infrastructure with energy-efficient (EE) lights based on LED technology [5,6]. It therefore follows that cities and municipalities require techno-economic analysis tools and methodologies that accurately forecast the likely viability of smart lighting projects.

The advent of a 'smart city' concept, with ubiquitous sensor and telecommunication networks, presents a good opportunity for implementation of smart lighting infrastructure [7]. A range of energy efficiency and demand-side management (EEDSM) activities that can be implemented on street lighting infrastructure include retrofitting of EE luminaires and implementation of advanced control systems such as smart lights [8]. Smart street lights incorporate sensor data-driven control systems to facilitate EE operations, optimized lighting performance and sometimes additional services to the residents [9,10].

Smart light systems use sensed information from traffic patterns to further reduce energy consumption. Sensors applied in recent literature include, timers in [6], proximity sensors in [7], received signal strength - based sensors in [9] and smart camera in [10]. Smart lights are shown to result in varying operating electricity cost reductions based on the amount of traffic [11]. Reported cost reduction rates vary from 15% in [11], through 30% in [10] and to 89.5% in [9].

Accurate techno-economic analysis of smart lighting projects needs to consider lighting performance, electricity tariffs, maintenance cost and the dynamic seasonal operating hours of streetlights [5,8]. The analysis' economic aspect should account for time-value-of-money by applying discounted cash flows because of the long time span of retrofit projects. Studies in Serbia [5], Turkey [6], Laramie - Unite State (US) [4] and El Cajon - US [12] resulted in a pay-back period of 2.83, 2.61, 4 and 3 years, respectively.

The street lighting performance depends on multiple road and street light pole parameters [11]. Thus, lighting simulation studies using software like AGi32 [4] and DIALux in [13,14] are needed for accurate energy modelling. Alternatively, photometric studies need to verify performance against local standards like EN13201 in [11,13].

Moreover, the maintenance cost calculations need to consider the varying life spans of different lighting technologies in order to anticipate the likely number of lights expected to fail per period, after installation. A comprehensive list of lamp burnout failure population decay models that can be used to accurately model the maintenance cost is given in [15]. However, many recently published techno-economic analysis studies like [4,5,8,11] ignore the lamp failure model.

Thus, the contribution of this paper is to presents a techno-economic analysis methodology for the assessment smart lighting retrofit project that incorporates the modeling of lamp failure rate to result in accurate maintenance cost calculations.

The paper is organized as follows. Section 2 explains the techno-economic analysis methodology. Section 3 applies the methodology on a case-study in South Africa and the conclusions are provided in Sect. 4.

2   Methodology

The analysis process begins with gathering of data from multiple sources as shown in Fig. 1. These includes both financial and technical data. Technical data includes, traffic information describing daily pattern of traffic, sun-set/rise times and measurements made on the streets. Measurements obtained from the streets include the total number of luminaires N_{tot}, the actual average power usage of the light, the size of the street, location of poles, pattern of poles, beam angle and over hang distance. The financial data gathered will be used for economic analysis. This data includes electricity price π_{elec} per kWh, unit purchase price of the luminaires or lamps π_{pur}, unit cost for installing a lighting fixture π_{inst}, and cost of replacing a lighting fixture π_{repl}. It is also important to gather data on the annual increases in electricity r_{elec}, maintenance r_{man} and discount rate d_r. Other data may include the rated lifetime of both the new and old lights, L.

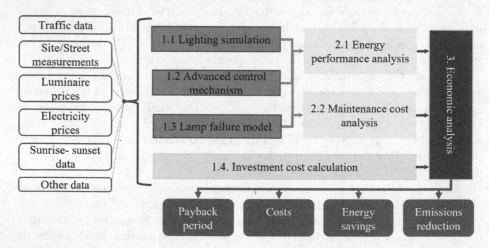

Fig. 1. Techno-economic analysis methodology

The street light measurement will be used to determine current total power usage of the lights P_{curr}. Step 1.1 identifies the most suitable replacement LED technology with its power rating P_{new}. The advanced control mechanism considered in step 1.2 will incorporate the currently installed photo-sensors and future traffic sensor data to dictate the dimming levels of new LED lights. Step 1.3 will determine the number of operating lights at each time period. In step 1.4, the investment cost is obtained by multiplying the installation and purchase price of luminaire units by their numbers given in (1).

$$C_{inv} = (\pi_{inst} + \pi_{pur}) N_{tot} \tag{1}$$

Thus, steps 1.1, 1.2 and 1.3 gives inputs to the energy performance analysis. The analysis can calculate the current monthly energy usage EB_i for month i, based on the number of days in that month D_i and the average operating hours, $\bar{h}_i$, calculated from sun-rise/set data. The advanced control signal $U_{control}$ is then used to compute the new monthly energy usage ER_i. The energy analysis calculation formulae are given in (3).

$$EB_i = P_{curr} \cdot D_i \cdot \bar{h}_i \text{ and } ER_i = P_{new}(U_{control}) \cdot D_i \cdot \bar{h}_i \tag{2}$$

$$ES_j = \sum_i^{12} EB_i - ER_i \tag{3}$$

The maintenance cost will depend on the number of lights that need to be maintained in a given period. The model adopted from [15] is used to calculate the number of failed lights, $N(t)$, according to (4).

$$N(t) = N_{tot} (1 - \Phi(t)), \text{ where } \Phi(t) = [c + exp(bt - L)]^{-1} \tag{4}$$

The lamp decay model, $\Phi(t)$, depends on modeling parameters c and b as wells as the rated lifetime L. According to [5], $L = 16000$ for HPS bulbs and 50000 for LED luminaires. The model $\Phi(t)$ gives a percentage of surviving lights after a time period t, thus by definition $\Phi(0) = 1$. Moreover by design, the model is calibrated so that half of the lamps have burnedout when $t = L$, thus $\Phi(L) = 0.5$. Therefore, knowing the value of L, this two facts can be used to easily determine parameters c and b by model fitting. It is worth noting that after replacement, the newly installed lights will decay at a different rate than the older already installed lights. Thus, multiple instances of the model, $\Phi(t)$, are required to keep track of the individual groups of lights with different ages.

The annual maintenance cost will depend on the number of lights needing replacement and the technology price π_{pur} as shown in 5.

$$C_{main}(t) = N(t) (\pi_{inst} + \pi_{pur}) \tag{5}$$

On the final step 3, in Fig. 1, the economic analysis is conducted to produces indices that can be used by decision makers within cities to determine the viability of projects. For smart lighting projects, the most common indices include pay-back period, net present value, energy savings, and annual CO_2 emission reductions [5,12,13]. In this case, we adopt a cost of ownership model of discounted costs over a period of M years as shown in (6).

$$CoM(M) = C_{inv} + \sum_{j=1}^{M} \left[-ES_j \cdot \pi_{elec} \cdot \frac{(1+r_{elec})^j}{(1+d_r)^j} \right.$$
$$\left. +(C_{main}^{old}(j) - C_{main}^{new}(j)) \cdot \frac{(1+r_{man})^j}{(1+d_r)^j} \right] \tag{6}$$

This analysis takes into account the energy and maintenance costs/savings made by retrofitting new luminaires on existing infrastructure. CoM also depends on discount rate d_r and annual increases in electricity price r_{elec} and maintenance costs r_{man}. The value of the annual savings, ES_j, is multiplied by price, π_{elec}, to get the energy cost savings. The value $(C_{main}^{old}(j) - C_{main}^{new}(j))$ is a calculation of cost savings on maintenance. The retrofit project is considered to have repaid its-self the moment, M, the CoM value becomes negative. This moment where the cost of ownership becomes negative is the payback point. The emission reductions can be calculated by multiplying the energy savings by an emission factor.

3   Results and Discussion

The application of the methodology proposed in Sect. 2 is implemented on a 4.2 km case-study road in Vanderbijlpark, South Africa. The road under consideration is show in Fig. 2. The analysis presented in this case-study shall consider three different scenarios, namely HPS, EE lights and smart lights. The HPS scenario maintains the status quo of installed HPS lights, the EE lights scenario simply retrofits HPS lamps with LED luminaires and the smart lights scenario adds the traffic-adaptive control and dimming controls to LED luminaires retrofits.

The road in Fig. 2 has a twin pole arrangement with poles located in the middle of two lanes. The site measurement of 11 m high poles, overreach of 2.5 m and carriageway width of 7 m are used to model the street in DIAlux simulation software as per step 1.1. The daylight duration data is gathered from [16].

Fig. 2. Case-study road in South Africa

Analysis shows that this is a class A3 road according to the standard [17]. The simulation results indicate that the currently installed 250 W HPS lights can be replaced with 180 W EE LED luminaires.

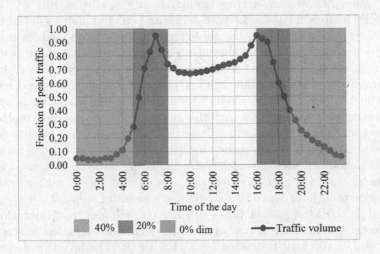

Fig. 3. Traffic based dimming schedule

The traffic data of the nearest city, Johannesburg, is used to analyse the likely traffic patterns on the road [18]. This analysis shows that the peak times for traffic are 7 am and 4 pm, during the weekdays. However, the traffic volumes are below 70% of the peak before 6 am in morning and after 6 pm in the evening, as illustrated in Fig. 3. Figure 3 also shows that there is very little traffic between the hours of 730 pm and 5 am the following morning (below 30%). These observations read together with SANS 10098 inspire the dimming schedule shown in Fig. 3, for evaluating the application of smart lights. Thus, the smart lights can operate at 60% of flux (or 40% dimming) from 730 pm to 5 am in the morning, at 100%

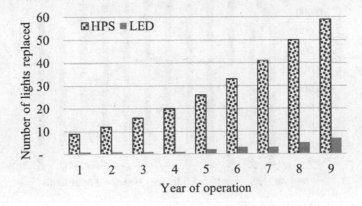

Fig. 4. Number of failed lamps/luminaires per annum

of flux from 6am to sunrise and from dusk to 6 pm. The rest of the time the lights will at 80% of flux, as shown in Fig. 3.

Figure 4 shows the number of lights requiring replacement. Based on the lifetime values, L, and an average annual hourly operating rate of 11.9 h, a typical HPS lamp will last for 3.7 years while an LED luminaire will last for 11.5 years. Given this information, the subsequent analysis is applied for a total of 9 years. The results of step 1.3 shown in Fig. 4 illustrate that there is minimal replacement required for LED luminaires, with only one replacement for each of the first 4 years. On the other hand as many as 9 HPS lights need replacing during the first year and this number rises to 40 in the year 7. It is apparent from the trend shown in Fig. 4 that the number of lights needing replacement increases with the age of the lamps. Thus, the maintenance cost calculated using (5), gives a more accurate estimation of the cost as opposed to using an average value throughout all the years of investment. Using an average annual value of maintenance cost will therefore over estimate of cost in the earlier years, and under estimate in later year. This analysis is a result of step 2.2.

Based on the local market prices of LED technologies from quotations and online stores, the investment cost of 104 LED lights is calculated in step 1.4 to be ZAR 382,720.00 for EE lighting ($\approx$ 21,409 USD). The investment cost price of smart lighting will include an added cost of cheap sensing infrastructure and dimming controllers [5]. An additional 10% is added to the investment cost to make a total of ZAR 459,264.00 ($\approx$ 25,691 USD). The unit purchase price and installation cost values used are $\pi_{pur} = 3,200$ and $\pi_{inst} = 480$, respectively.

The results of step 2.1 are shown in Fig. 5. Applying (3) results in a total annual energy usage of 131 MWh for the HPS, 81.6 MWh for EE lights and 78.6 MWh for smart lights. The results in Fig. 5 show that the energy usage of street lights is highest during winter months of May, June and July when

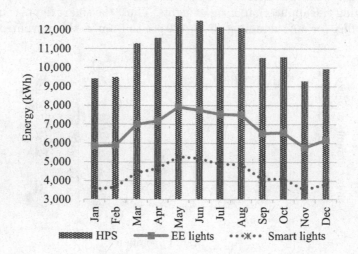

Fig. 5. Simulated monthly energy usage

daytime is shorter in the Southern hemisphere, as expected. It can also be seen from Fig. 5 that, while EE lights seem to save almost half of the HPS energy consumption, the smart lights perform even better.

Economic analysis in step 3 applies (6) for a total of $M = 9$ years. The results of the cumulative sum of the discounted cash-flows is shown in Fig. 6. Linearly extrapolating the results in Fig. 6 shows that EE lights have a payback period of 4.26 years, while smart lights have a payback period of 3.42 years. These figures are relatively high but comparable to the values obtained in other studies from US, Serbia and Turkey [4–6,12]. The payback period also depends on electricity pricing. The assessment currently considers only the energy rate of a single tariff offered by Eskom, a public utility supplying the majority of municipalities in South Africa [19].

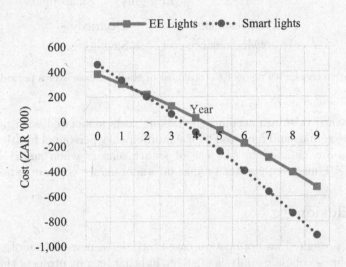

Fig. 6. Cost of ownership - cumulative sum of discounted cash flows

Figure 7 shows the cost components and savings of the different scenarios relative to the total cost of the HPS scenario. The maintenance cost accounts for a small, 10%, portion of the overall cost in the HPS scenario. However, comparing the HPS and the two retrofit scenarios shows that the LED retrofit does provide maintenance cost savings. The 5% increase in investment cost when moving from EE lights to smart lights is shown to result in a significant increase in savings, by more than 10%. Using a simple annual average value, without the model in (4), results in the under estimation of maintenance cost by a factor 4 in the first year and 25 by the 9th year, for the HPS scenario. This underestimates the annual savings on maintenance cost leading to a 6 months delay in payback period calculations for EE lights. This deviation is likely to be significant when the cost of maintenance is modeled more accurately so that it becomes significant in the overall operating cost of streetlights. The currently proposed cost model does

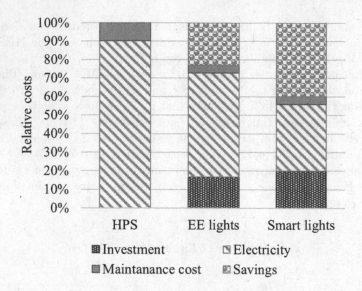

Fig. 7. Relative costs with respect to total cost of the base case over a period of 9 years

not for instance take into account the labour costs associated with performing maintenance rounds and fuel used by the municipality personnel to drive around. These costs are nullified by the use of smart sensors when smart lights are deployed [7]. Thus, even greater savings on maintenance cost are expected.

4   Conclusion

This paper presented an application case-study for a new methodology of performing techno-economic analysis of street lighting retrofit projects that involve energy-efficient lights and smart lights using traffic-adaptive control. The proposed methodology is generic and can be applied to cities in any country in the world using appropriate case-study data. The case-study area applied currently has HPS lamps that are switched by photo sensors. The methodology presented aims to offer an accurate assessment using lighting simulations, considering seasonal variations of light operating hours, a lamp failure model to inform maintenance cost calculations and discounted cash flows. The application of the proposed model resulted in a payback periods of 3.42 and 4.26 years, for smart lights and EE lights retrofits, respectively. The current modeling of maintenance cost is shown to improve the economic evaluation. Future work in this area needs to consider a more thorough modeling of maintenance costs, evaluations of streets where timing control is used, the impact of dimming level on pedestrian safety and detailed analysis of the electricity pricing tariffs.

References

1. Angelopulo, G.: A comparative measure of inclusive urbanisation in the cities of Africa. World Dev. Perspect. **22**, 100313 (2021). https://doi.org/10.1016/j.wdp.2021.100313

2. Liu, Q., Cheng, K., Zhuang, Y.: Estimation of city energy consumption in China based on downscaling energy balance tables. Energy **256**, 124658 (2022). https://doi.org/10.1016/j.energy.2022.124658

3. Shahzad, G., Yang, H., Ahmad, A.W., Lee, C.: Energy-efficient intelligent street lighting system using traffic-adaptive control. IEEE Sens. J. **16**(13), 5397–5405 (2016). https://doi.org/10.1109/JSEN.2016.2557345.2021;22:100313

4. Akindipe, A., Olawale, O.W., Bujko, R.: Effect of environmental and social responsibility in energy-efficient management models for smart cities infrastructure. Sustain. Cities Soc. **84**, 103989 (2022). https://doi.org/10.1016/j.scs.2022.103989

5. Gordic, D., Vukasinovic, V., Kovacevic, Z., Josijevic, M., Zivkovic, D.: Assessing the techno-economic effects of replacing energy-inefficient street lighting with LED corn bulbs. Energies **14**, 3755 (2021). https://doi.org/10.3390/en14133755

6. Gorgulu, S., Kocabey, S.: An energy saving potential analysis of lighting retrofit scenarios in outdoor lighting systems: a case study for a university campus. J. Clean. Prod. **260**, 121060 (2020). https://doi.org/10.1016/j.jclepro.2020.121060

7. Rahman, M.A., Asyhari, A.T., Obaidat, M.S., Kurniawan, I.F., Mukta, M.Y., Vijayakumar, P.: IoT-enabled light intensity-controlled seamless highway lighting system. IEEE Syst. J. **15**(1), 46–55 (2021). https://doi.org/10.1109/JSYST.2020.2975592

8. Xia, X., Wu, X., BalaMurugan, S., Karuppiah, M.: Effect of environmental and social responsibility in energy-efficient management models for smart cities infrastructure. Sustain Energy Technol Assess **47**, 101525 (2021). https://doi.org/10.1016/j.seta.2021.101525

9. Jiang, Y., Shuai, Y., He, X., Wen, X., Lou, L.: An energy-efficient street lighting approach based on traffic parameters measured by wireless sensing technology. IEEE Sens. J. **17**(17), 19134–43 (2021). https://doi.org/10.1109/JSEN.2021.3089208

10. Chiradeja, P., Yoomak, S., Ngaopitakkul, A.: Economic analysis of improving the energy efficiency of nanogrid solar road lighting using adaptive lighting control. IEEE Access **8**, 202623–38 (2020). https://doi.org/10.1109/JSEN.2021.3089208

11. Fryc, I., Czyzewski, D., Fan, J., Galatanu, C.D.: The drive towards optimization of road lighting energy consumption based on Mesopic vision-a suburban street case study. Energies **14**, 1175 (2021). https://doi.org/10.3390/en14041175

12. Viswanathan, S., Momand, S., Fruten, S., Alcantar, A.: A model for the assessment of energy-efficient smart street lighting-a case study. Energ. Effi. **14**(52), 2–20 (2021). https://doi.org/10.1007/s12053-021-09957-w

13. Duman, A.C., Guler, O.: Techno-economic analysis of off-grid photovoltaic LED road lighting systems: a case study for northern, central and southern regions of Turkey. Build. Environ. **156**, 89–98 (2019). https://doi.org/10.1016/j.buildenv.2019.04.005

14. DIALux evo 10.1 (2022). http://www.dialux.com. Accessed 10 Jun 2022

15. Ikuzwe, A., Xia, X., Ye, X.: Maintenance optimization incorporating lumen degradation failure for energy-efficient lighting retrofit projects. Appl. Energy **267**, 115003 (2020). https://doi.org/10.1016/j.apenergy.2020.115003

16. Sunrise and Sunset Calculator (2022). http://www.timeanddate.com/sun/. Accessed 10 Jun 2022
17. South African Bureau of Standards. Standard SANS-10098-1: Public lighting Part 1-The lighting of public thoroughfares. Pretoria, South Africa (2003)
18. TomTom. Traffic hourly congestion level data (2022). http://www.tomtom.com/en_gb/traffic-index/johannesburg-traffic/. Accessed 10 Jun 2022
19. Eskom. Schedule of standard prices for Eskom Tariffs (2022). http://www.eskom.co.za/distribution/wp-content/uploads/2022/04/Tariff-Booklet-final.pdf. Accessed 10 Jun 2022

Power Quality; Power Electronics

Development of a Smart Energy Meter for Electrical Energy Consumption and Power

Amira Haddouk[(⊠)], Asma Tanazafti, and Hfaiedh Mechergui

Department of Electrical Engineering, ENSIT University of Tunis, Tunis, Tunisia
{amira.haddouk,hafiedh.mechergui}@ensit.rnu.tn

Abstract. In this paper, the method of parameters measurement and identification of non linear load, using a Smart Energy Meter (SEM), is proposed. Currently, most loads are non-linear containing harmonics when connected to the electrical network. Most modern electricity meter algorithms take these harmonics into account, but with flaws. The proposed system in this paper replaces the traditional meter. The reading method and the communication module are based on the Node MCU ESP8266 WiFi module, a PIC18F4550 microcontroller and the results (active power P, deformation factor D and the active energy We) are displayed and illustrated by graphs on LabView. An LCD displays the numerical values of power and energy.

Keywords: Non linear load · Distortion Power Ratio (DPR) · Smart Energy Meter (SEM) · Energy consumption · Measurements · Transducers · Uncertainty

1 Introduction

Households are poorly informed about how they use electricity and their environmental impact. Since electricity is invisible, consumers often have trouble understanding when they over-consume [16, 18]. Informational feedback appeared as an instrument responding to this need to identify and understand the foundations of electricity consumption [11, 12, 19, 20].

For example, the electricity bill is a document reflecting a simple transaction (sale of electricity), where the supplier sells kWh to a buyer who does not understand on what basis the said transaction is invoiced, if this is only the electricity he has consumed is not billed at the same price depending on when he called it, consumption being billed in instalments, when subscribers have not taken out a single rate contract where kWh is sold at the same price regardless of the time of day it is consumed. In addition, simply reading the consumption indexes appearing on the electricity bill does not allow the consumer [12, 15, 17] to clearly identify the nature of the changes required or to link the reduction in the consumption of equipment to a change in behavior [5, 8, 11, 16].

Indeed, in [1, 2, 20], it is shown the inadequacy of smart meter to monitor and measure power quality phenomena due to high harmonic content. By the way the actual

J. L. Afonso et al. (Eds.): SESC 2022, LNICST 502, pp. 69–78, 2023.
https://doi.org/10.1007/978-3-031-33979-0_7

smart energy meter [6, 7, 14] do not deal with the quality of the load in a precise way but they are interested in billing in order to reduce energy consumption and costs.

Thus, a lot of parameters are not analyzed especially the distortion factor which informs us on the degree of nonlinearity of the load [9]. In fact, the consumer does not know about the extra energy consumption because they do not know how to calculate electrical energy that has been used in their house.

As a contribution to solve these issues, can come from the measuring and controlling the Distortion Power Ratio (DPR), to determine the behaviour of the AC electronic equipment Keeping the above issues in mind, we worked on the development of a smart energy meter (SEM) having the ability to measure, process and store the data while remaining in standby to track the fluctuations of the power consumed by the various loads [21]. In fact, this process will allow the customer to have a real idea of his consumption in order to control, if necessary, the excess in electrical energy and this via the identification of the quality factor of the installation and which reflects the behavior of the pollution load.

The performance of the developed SEM was investigated under non-sinusoidal conditions. The SEM is embedded with a PIC18F4550 microcontroller. It is programmed to measure instantaneous and an aggregation of real time total active power consumed; the power due to the first harmonic, the distortion factor, power factor and the consumed energy, then sends it to a PC through the NodeMCU ESP8266. Finally, after processing the collected data, the results are presented using an instrumental LabView platform. This paper proposes a new idea to measure the distortion power ratio DPR easily, in order to improve energy consumption and does not affect the power grid. In fact, by measuring the DPR it is possible to control the current harmonic distortion, and minimize energy consumption by controlling the pollutant load.

The rest of the paper is organized as follows. Section 2 presents the proposed solution for the smart energy meter, Sect. 3 illustrates the approaches and concept design, Sect. 4 introduces the mathematical analysis and Sect. 5 presents the conclusions.

2 Proposed Solution Used for the Smart Energy Meter

In this work, we develop a smart energy meter which measures energy, the active and reactive power and identifies load parameters in order to control energy consumption. The strategy used to measure the total active power is following described.

In the case of non-linear conditions with a non-sinusoidal source supply, voltage and current have the following respective expressions:

$$v(t) = \sum_{j=1}^{\infty} V_j \sqrt{2} \sin(j\omega t) \text{ and } i(t) = \sum_{j=1}^{\infty} I_j \sqrt{2} \sin(j\omega t + \phi_j) \tag{1}$$

where j is the harmonic order.

From expression (1) we deduce the active power:

$$P = V_1 I_1 \cos\phi_1 + V_2 I_2 \cos\phi_2 + \dots V_j I_j \cos\phi_j = V_1 I_1 \cos\varphi_1 + \sum_{j=2}^{\infty} V_j I_j \cos\phi_j \tag{2}$$

And

$$Q = Q_1 + Q_2 + \dots Q_j = \sum_{j=1}^{\infty} V_j I_j \sin \phi_j$$

So the power factor is given as:

$$PF = \frac{P}{S} = \frac{\sum_{j=1}^{\infty} V_j I_j \cos \phi_j}{\sqrt{\left(V_1^2 + \sum_{j=2}^{\infty} V_j^2\right)} \times \sqrt{\left(I_1^2 + \sum_{j=2}^{\infty} I_j^2\right)}} \tag{3}$$

In the case of a non-linear load, the distorting power can be written as:

$$D = \sqrt{\sum_{j=2}^{\infty} V_j^2 \times I_j^2} \tag{4a}$$

We note that D depends on the total harmonic of the current load and voltage network. In general, the voltage network is sinusoidal and the current load is non linear, so we can write:

$P \approx VI_1 \cos \varphi_1$ and $Q \approx VI_1 \sin \varphi_1$ so the deformed power is:

$$D \approx V \times \sqrt{\sum_{j=2}^{\infty} I_j^2} \tag{4b}$$

From the Eq. (4.b) we note that more the current is distorted more the Joule losses increase and this will affect the electric cables [13].

3 Approaches and Concept Design

The advantages presented by electronic energy meters are by far those of electromechanical meters. Indeed, modern energy measurement techniques have good reproducibility and are immune to noise. In addition, they take into account the distorting power. They use intelligent systems that deal with algorithms involving digital filtering calculations.

In our work, we have associated, upstream, a PIC18F4550 with a Node MCU ESP8266 module allowing the transfer of data to an instrumental platform managed by LabView. The microcontroller has also been associated with current and voltage Hall effect sensors with their conditioners and an LCD circuit ensuring the display of power and energy.

So we can calculate, V_{RMS}, I_{RMS}, $I_{1\text{-}RMS}$, the total active power consumed and the power due to the first harmonic P_1.

The whole working will be monitored and reported to the user by using a 16x2 LCD display.

An ESP8266 modules comes with a default firmware loaded into it, hence we can program the module using AT commands. These commands have to be sent through a serial communication channel. This channel is established between the PIC and the ESP8266 module by using the USART module in the PIC microcontroller.

The system communicates with an instrumental platform which makes all analysis to control the consumed energy taking into account the signature of the charge (Fig. 1).

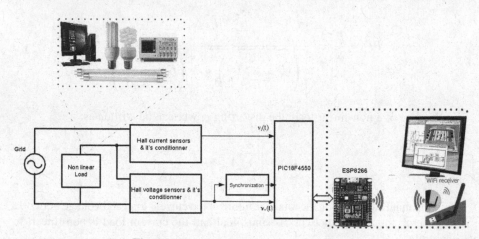

Fig. 1. Block diagram of the proposed SEM.

4   Mathematical Analyses

In general, to measure the active power, we multiply the outputs of the signal conditioning circuits $v_v(t)$ and $v_i(t)$.

For a non linear load the active power, which is also called real power; in fact the average value of the instantaneous power $p_h(t)$ is given by

$$p(t) = \frac{1}{T} \int_0^T v(t) \cdot i(t) dt$$

$$= \frac{1}{T} \left(\int_0^T \sum_{h=1}^{\infty} [V_{hm} \sin(h\omega t) \cdot I_{hm} \sin(h\omega t + \varphi_h)] dt \right) \tag{5}$$

According to (2) and (5), the total harmonic distortion is defined by (6):

$$THD_P = \frac{\sum_{h=2}^{\infty} P_h}{P_1} \tag{6}$$

We define the distortion power ratio DPR as follow:

$$DPR = \frac{P_1}{P} = \frac{P_1}{P_1 + \sum_{h=2}^{\infty} P_h} \tag{7}$$

It is assumed that THD_P tend to zero, the Eq. (7) can be written as:

$$DPR \cong 1 - THD_P \tag{8}$$

In some cases, the voltage supplying a non-linear load is non-sinusoidal. This leads to a harmonic distortion of current and voltage, which degrades the distorting power D. To determine the various electrical quantities necessary for the measurement of active and reactive power, energy and the deformation factor, then, the current flowing through the load and the voltage across are acquired periodically.

Let $v_v(n)$ and $v_i(n)$ be respectively the digitized waveforms of the analog $v_v(t)$ and $v_i(t)$ during one period T_g, of the power grid. Thus we can write: $v_n = k_v v(nT_e)$ and $i_n = k_v v_i(nT_e)$.

k_v: scaling factor for the voltage

k_i: scaling factor for the current

T_e: sampling period

T_g: grid period.

Having acquired over one period the N samples of $v_{v\text{-}acq}$ and $v_{i\text{-}acq}$, we calculate, respectively, the effective value of the RMS value of the voltage and the current:

$$v_{vacq} = V_{dc} + v_v(t) \text{ and } v_{iacq} = V_{dc} + v_i(t) \tag{9}$$

To extract $v_v(t)$ and $v_i(t)$, it is necessary to read sampled data from each ADC and store it in location in the static Random access memory(SRAM), where it cannot be over written by new data.

To remove the DC offset we need more calculations, so the best solution is to use a digital High-Pass Filter (HPF) of type infinite impulse response (IIR). According to the transfer function of the filter can be written as follows:

$$y[(n)] = 0.996 \times y[n-1] + 0.996 \times x[n] - 0.996 \times x[n-1] \tag{10}$$

This digital filter is simple one and it removes the DC offset.

Then we calculate V_{rms} and I_{rms}.

To increase the accuracy of the used method, the measurement operations are performed over a time noted T_M such as:

$$T_M = M \times T_g \tag{11}$$

where M is the integer that is a multiple of the period T_g. Then, we calculate a rated power P_t, and the expression (11) can be written as follows:

$$P_M = \frac{1}{M} \sum_{j=1}^{M} P_N \tag{12}$$

The consumed energy is then calculated based on the active power value for each frame of one second, that means:

$$\Delta W_e = P_M \times \Delta t (1 \sec ond) \tag{13}$$

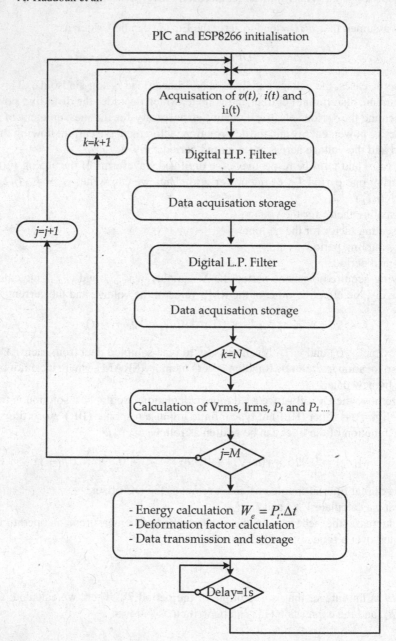

Fig. 2. General flow chart

To calculate the power P1 due to the first harmonic of the current, we use, also, a digital low pass filter, so can write:

$$P_1 = \frac{1}{k_P} \cdot \frac{1}{M} \left(\sum_{j=1}^{M} \frac{1}{N} \left(\sum_{n=1}^{N} v_{v_1}(n) \cdot v_{i_1}(n) \right) \right) \tag{14}$$

Making recourse to Eq. (2) and (14), we determine the behavior of the load. The flow chart of the SEM is depicted in Fig. 2.

Figure 3 presents the implemented hardware of the SEM.

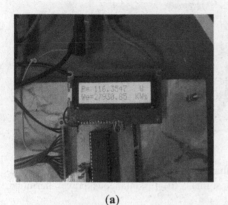
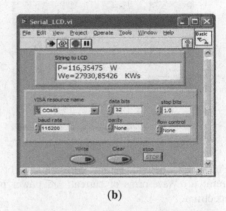

(a)   (b)

Fig. 3. Experimental setup: (**a**) Experimental results displayed in LCD; (**b**) Experimental results transmitted and displayed on the Labview.

• *Practical identification of the current consumed by a non-linear load (example: power supply model PR-657).*

Experimental tests were carried out on a non-linear load (PR-657 type laboratory power supply). From the spectral analysis, it can be seen that the load current is much distorted, which has an impact on the voltage shape at the contact point at the network connection. The Fig. 4 and Fig. 5 illustrates also the behavior of the currents across the load and the instantaneous power consumed.

The designed energy meter has been tested in our instrumentation laboratory. Indeed, the latter contains electrical appliances similar to those of a dwelling house. We took measurements, during a week, according to the objective presented in this work. Thus, the collected data is processed and analyzed by a LabView platform. The results of the analysis showed that the nonlinear behavior of the load affects the stability and pollution of the network voltage and consequently increases the losses.

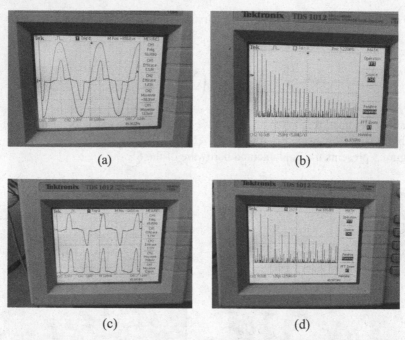

(a)   (b)

(c)   (d)

Fig. 4. Experimental curves: (a) waveforms of voltage and current; (b) Current harmonic spectrum; (c) Waveforms of current and power p(t) signals; (d) Instantaneous power harmonic spectrum

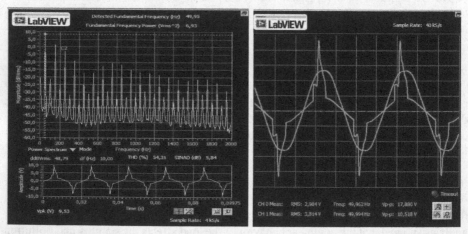

Fig. 5. Real time acquisition of current/voltage signals and spectral analysis: case of a non- linear load (compact fluorescent lamp 25 W)

5 Conclusions

This paper presents the design and implementation of an intelligent energy meter (SEM) that can be used in the home with the possibility of real-time energy measurement and the determination of the deformation factor in order to control the load affecting excessive electrical energy consumption. This system has the flexibility and ability to be modified and manipulated to suit various environments of electrical load combinations. The SEM uses modern digital techniques which are acquisition, digital filter processing and data transmission via WiFi.

A platform managed by LabView allows the processing, calculation, analysis and representation of consumption curves, the purpose of which is to validate the use of the smart energy meter in the housing sector.

The spectral analysis carried out showed that modern electronic devices (using semi-conductors) are highly non-linear loads which the SEM carried out can intervene to control the latter so as not to affect the network voltage.

References

1. Ayari, A., Mechergui, H., Haddouk, A.: Active power measurement comparison between analog and digital methods. In: International Conference on Electrical Engineering and Software Applications (ICEESA), Hammamet - Tunisia, 21 – 23 March 2013 (2013). ISBN: 978-1-4673-6302-0, https://doi.org/10.1109/ICEESA.2013.6578416
2. Ayari, A.: Contribution au développement des méthodes de mesure de puissances active, réactive pour des charges linéaires et non linéaires et Optimisation de l'énergie, Ph.D., ENSIT, University of Tunis - Tunisia, 16 May (2015)
3. Ayari, A., et al.: Design and implementation of Single Phase Intelligent Energy Meter using a microcontroller interfaced to PC, 15th International conference on Sciences and Techniques Automatic control and computer engineering, STA'2014, December 21–23, Hammamet, Tunisia, 978-1-4799-5906-8/14/$31.00 ©2014, pp. 191–195. IEEE Conference Publications (2014)
4. ANEEL: General Condicions for Electrical Energy Supply (in Portuguese), Resolution 414/2010 (2010)
5. Bartolomei, L., et al.: 'Testing of electrical energy meters subject to realistic distorted voltages and currents. Energies 13, 2023 (2020). https://doi.org/10.3390/en13082023
6. Benqiang, Y., et al.: Smart metering and systems for low-energy households: challenges, issues and benefits. Adv. Build. Energy Res. 13(1), 80–100 (2019). https://doi.org/10.1080/17512549.2017.1354782
7. Darby, S.: Smart metering: what potential for householder engagement? pp: 442–457 (2010). | Published online: 25 Aug 2010, https://doi.org/10.1080/09613218.2010.492660
8. Gheorghe Beleiu, H., et al.: Management of power quality issues from an economic point of view. Sustainability 10(7), 2326 (2018). https://doi.org/10.3390/su10072326
9. Gianluca, A., et al.: AC electronic load for on-site calibration of energy meters. In: IEEE Instrumentation and Measurement Technology Conference (2013). https://doi.org/10.1109/I2MTC.2013.6555519
10. Hlaili, M.: Development and control of power electronics for a photovoltaic power generation system for on-grid off-grid operation, Ph.D., ENSIT, University of Tunis - Tunisia, 21 January (2017)

11. Harrison, A.: The Effects of Harmonics on Power Quality and Energy Efficiency Technological, University Dublin, Bachelor of Science in Electrical Services and Energy Management (2010)
12. Khlifi, K., et al.: Harmonic pollution caused by non-linear load: analysis and identification. Int. J. Energy Environ. Eng. **12**, 510–517 (2018)
13. Khlifi, K.: Gestion de l'énergie électrique dans l'habitat intégrant les charges non linéaires, Ph.D, ENSIT, University of Tunis - Tunisia, 27 February (2021)
14. Kuralkar, P. et al.: Smart Energy Meter: Applications, Bibliometric Reviews and Future Research Directions Saloni, pp:165–188 (2020). Published online: 17 Apr 2020 https://doi.org/10.1080/0194262X.2020.1750081
15. Ouyang S. and Xuntao, S.: The analysis of power meters performance under non sinusoidal conditions. In: International Conference on Power System Technology (2010). 978-1-4244-5940-7110/$26.00© IEEE
16. Rönnberg, S., Bollen, M.: Power quality issues in the electric power system of the future'. Electr. J. **29**(10), 49–61 (2016). https://doi.org/10.1016/j.tej.2016.11.006
17. Olivares-Rojas. J.C., Reyes-Archundia, E., Gutiérrez-Gnecchi, J.A., González-Murueta, J.W., Cerda-Jacobo, J.: A multi-tier architecture for data analytics in smart metering systems. Simul Model Pract Theory 102024 (2019)
18. Mbungu, N., Naidoo, R., Bansal, R., Bipath, M.: Grid integration and optimization through smart metering. In: 2nd SAIEE Smart Grid Conference, Midrand, South Africa, pp. 19–21 (2017)
19. Weranga, K., Kumarawadu, S., Chandima, D.: Smart metering design and applications. Springer, Heidelberg, Germany (2014)
20. Mbungu, N.T., Naidoo, R.M., Bansal, R.C., Vahidinasab, V.: Overview of the optimal smart energy coordination for microgrid applications. IEEE Access **7**, 163063–163084 (2019)
21. Ajanovic, A., Hiesl, A., Haas, R.: On the role of storage for electricity in smart energy systems, Energy 117473 (2020)

A Hybrid MPPT Algorithm Based on DE-IC for Photovoltaic Systems Under Partial Shading Conditions

Rafaela D. Silveira[1]([⊠]), Sérgio A. O. da Silva[1], Leonardo P. Sampaio[1], and Jose A. Afonso[2,3]

[1] Federal University of Technology, Cornélio Procópio, PR 86300-000, Brazil
rafaeladsilveira@hotmail.com, {augus,sampaio}@utfpr.edu.br
[2] CMEMS – UMinho, University of Minho, 4800-058 Guimarães, Portugal
jose.afonso@dei.uminho.pt
[3] LABBELS – Associate Laboratory, Braga/Guimarães, Portugal

Abstract. This paper presents a hybrid maximum power point tracking (MPPT), which combines a metaheuristic algorithm and a traditional MPPT method applied in a photovoltaic system operating under partial shading conditions. The MPPTs based on traditional methods are not able to track the global maximum power point (GMPP) when partial shadings occur. Thus, MPPT algorithms based on metaheuristic algorithms, which are used for global optimization, have presented efficiency to extract the maximum power from photovoltaic arrays. However, these methods are random, resulting in large power oscillations in transients of small variations in solar irradiance. Therefore, this paper proposes the metaheuristic algorithm called Differential Evolution (DE) to seek and track the GMPP. After the DE convergence, the MPPT algorithm is switched to Incremental Conductance (IC) in order to refine the tracking. The effectiveness of the algorithm is proved through simulation results. Furthermore, comparative analyses are provided for each algorithm (DE and IC) to evaluate their performances in the PV system.

Keywords: Photovoltaic System · Maximum Power Point Tracking · Differential Evolution · Incremental Conductance

1 Introduction

In the past years, power generators based on new renewable energy resources, such as wind, solar, and fuel cells, have been considered prominent solutions to complement the demand for energy supply and overcome environmental issues [1]. In particular, the solar energy resource, using photovoltaic (PV) generators, has been distinguished due to its availability, noise-free, easy installation, and low maintenance [2]. Therefore, PV systems are seen to be suitable for adoption in the distributed generation modality as well as in autonomous applications.

© ICST Institute for Computer Sciences, Social Informatics and Telecommunications Engineering 2023
Published by Springer Nature Switzerland AG 2023. All Rights Reserved
J. L. Afonso et al. (Eds.): SESC 2022, LNICST 502, pp. 79–91, 2023.
https://doi.org/10.1007/978-3-031-33979-0_8

Several research studies have discussed the assessment of efficiency and performance for PV systems developing proper technologies and materials according to the application [3–5]. On the other hand, PV systems deal with non-linear electrical characteristics, which are influenced by weather conditions such as solar irradiance and temperature, which means that the power produced by PV modules, is weather-dependent [2]. Nevertheless, since the output power-voltage (P-V) characteristic curve of a PV array has a maximum power point (MPP), appropriate maximum power point tracking (MPPT) techniques can be employed to maximize the overall system efficiency [2].

Under uniform solar irradiance, the MPP can accurately be tracked by using traditional MPPTs, such as Perturb and Observe (P&O), Incremental Conductance (IC), constant-voltage tracing, and Beta [3]. However, when partial shading conditions occur, the PV array can be exposed to different levels of solar irradiance, which can limit its power generation. [5]. To mitigate this effect, bypass diodes can be used across the PV modules to protect them and provide alternatives path for the currents. Consequently, with this strategy, the P-V curve exhibits multiple local MPP (LMPP) and only one global MPP (GMPP), making the tracking more challenging for the traditional methods, which may not be able to differentiate the LMPPs from the GMPP, resulting in power losses [4–6].

To overcome the problems associated with partial shading conditions, as well as with the LMPPs and GMPPs, a large number of MPPT algorithms based on meta-heuristic methods, have been proposed in the literature, such as particle swarm optimization [5], ant colony optimizer, bat search algorithm, grey wolf optimization (GWO), whale optimization, genetic algorithms, among others [5, 7]. Some research reviews on these MPPT techniques have been undertaken to compare their performances related to convergence-time, computational efforts, and power oscillations [6–9].

In general, despite the effectiveness on seek the GMPP, the inherent drawback of the meta-heuristics MPPTs consists of randomness. Once they need to perform the whole search space on the P-V curve, even minimal changes in solar irradiance imply large power oscillations. To overcome this drawback, hybrid methods, that combine two or more algorithms, have great potential that can be explored in more detail [8].

In this context, among the several existing meta-heuristic algorithms, the differential-evolution (DE), based on genetic algorithm, has been highlighted [10–12]. The DE algorithm can be used for global optimization to obtain the solution for practical problems which have noncontinuous and nonlinear characteristics or have many local minima or constraints [11]. Moreover, DE requires few for fine-tuning. The research work depicted in [10], relies upon DE to perform the MPPT in a partial shading PV system, however, large power oscillations were obtained and the effect caused by minimal changes in solar irradiance was not evaluated.

In this paper, a combined algorithm is proposed incorporating the DE and IC methods, resulting in a hybrid MPPT technique. Firstly, the DE method performs the GMPP tracking, when achieving the convergence, the IC method acts to avoid large power oscillations in steady-state. Therefore, tracking efficiency, convergence time, and accuracy can be improved with the hybrid algorithm (DE-IC), in comparison with their versions implemented only as DE or as IC. To evaluate the performance, the MPPT algorithm is applied to a PV system composed of a PV array, a dc-dc boost converter, and a resistive load. Moreover, comparative analysis considering the MPPTs based on IC, DE, and DE-IC is provided by means of computational analysis.

2 PV System Description

The electrical power circuit of the PV system implemented in this paper is presented in Fig. 1. The system consists of a PV array composed of four series-connected PV modules, resulting in a power generation around to 980 W at standard test conditions (STC). A dc-dc boost converter is employed to interface the PV array and the load.

In the referred PV system, the MPPT algorithm is carried out by the control system of the dc-dc boost converter. The dc-dc boost converter is controlled by using two control loops, as presented in Fig. 1. A voltage loop is adopted to control the PV array voltage (v_{pv}), whose voltage reference is provided by the MPPT algorithm, while an inner current control loop is employed to control the boost inductor current (i_{Lb}), whose reference is obtained from the voltage loop.

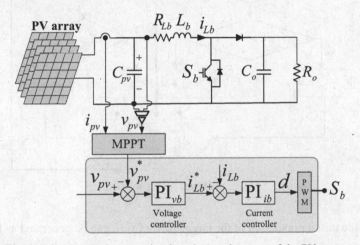

Fig. 1. The electrical power circuit and control system of the PV system.

3 MPPT Techniques

The IC method is based on detecting the slope of the characteristic P-V curve. The power slope of the PV array is null at MPP (dP/dV = 0), as well as positive on the left, and negative on the right of the curve [3]. Thus, due to this condition, this algorithm can track the MPP by using the increment in the array conductance. Therefore, the algorithm tends to change the reference values, in this case, the voltage reference (v_{pv}^*), according to a pre-defined fixed increment step always seeking to remain in the maximum point. The flowchart of the IC implemented as MPPT is represented in Fig. 2.

On the other hand, the DE is a metaheuristic algorithm classified as an evolutionary method, which was proposed by Storn and Price for global optimization [12]. The DE works on creating a target vector to represent a population of individuals. In order to achieve the problem solution, a few interactions are needed to submit the created population to the following genetic operators: mutation, crossover, and selection [10, 12]. Thus, for each interaction, the evolved individuals are evaluated as a possible solution until an attained satisfactory criterion or a termination condition.

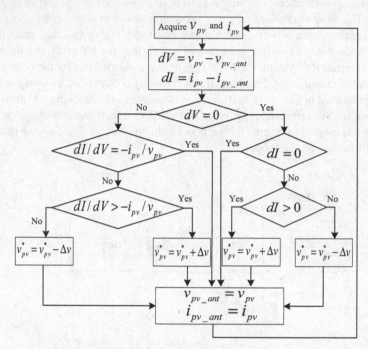

Fig. 2. IC-based MPPT method.

Thus, the initial population of the target vectors $x_{i,G}$, can be generated as follows:

$$x_{i,G}, i = 1, 2, 3 \ldots NP \tag{1}$$

where NP is the total number of individuals and the index G is the vector's generation.

After that, three target vectors are randomly selected to the mutation process, which works by using a mutation factor to provide a weighted difference between two target vectors. Then, the weighted difference is added to the third target vector to obtain the mutant vector $v_{i,G+1}$, as given by:

$$v_{i,G+1} = x_{1,G} + F(x_{2,G} - x_{3,G}) \tag{2}$$

where $x_{1,G}, x_{2,G}$ and $x_{3,G}$ are the selected target vectors and F is the mutation factor usually chosen in the range of [0,2]. This process can be associated with the advantage through competition between the individuals, where each individual in a community is learning from the difference between each other and generates the better individual in order to ensure the promotion of the community.

In sequence, the crossover operation is introduced in the DE in order to promote diversity among mutant vectors. Therefore, the mutant vectors $v_{i,G+1}$ when combined with target vectors $(x_{i,G})$, can generates trial vectors $u_{i,G+1}$, according to the condition:

$$u_{i,G+1} = \begin{cases} v_{1,G+1}, & \text{if } rand_i \leq C_r \\ x_{1,G+1}, & rand_i > C_r \end{cases} \tag{3}$$

where a random number $rand_i$ in the range of $[0, 1]$ is compared with the crossover rate C_r, which is a control variable in the range of $[0,1]$.

After the results of the crossover process, the trial vector is evaluated in a fitness function, which is associated with the problem statement. If the trial vector performs the best solution when compared with the target vector, then the trial vector is used as the target vector for the next generation. This operation is the selection and can be described as:

$$x_{i,G+1} = \begin{cases} u_{1,G+1}, & f_{fitness}(u_{1,G+1}) < f_{fitness}(x_{1,G}) \\ x_{1,G}, & otherwise \end{cases} \tag{4}$$

In this paper, as previously mentioned, the MPPT algorithm provides the reference voltage to the control system of the dc-dc boost converter. Thus, considering the DE to the MPPT application, the target vectors are equivalent to the PV array reference voltages, and the solutions resulting from each iteration are equivalent to the PV array output power. Therefore, the initialization of the target vector in (1) can be rewritten in the proposed DE-MPPT algorithm as follows:

$$v_{pvi}^*, i = 1, 2, 3 \ldots NP \tag{5}$$

where $v_{pvi,G}^*$ represents the PV array reference voltages as target vectors.

The global best solution is obtained by comparing all the solutions for the NP reference voltages. In this case, the PV array power is considered as the solution, in which the highest power is selected as the best solution, and its corresponding v_{pvi}^* is considered as the best individual $v_{pv\_best}^*$ of such population. The flowchart of the DE-MPPT is presented in Fig. 3.

In certain cases, the performances of the meta-heuristic algorithms can be affected under small variations of solar irradiance, resulting in large power oscillations. To overcome this problem, this work proposes to combine both techniques (DE and IC) to take advantage of each one through a hybrid algorithm. The proposed hybrid technique can improve the performance in GMPP tracking under conditions that resemble practical applications. Firstly, the DE method performs the GMPP tracking, when achieving the convergence, the IC method acts to avoid large power oscillations in steady-state. Figure 4 presents the flowchart of the hybrid algorithm DE-IC developed in this paper.

4 Simulation Results

The effectiveness of the presented MPPT techniques was evaluated by means of simulation results using MATLAB/Simulink computational tool. Table 1 presents the electrical characteristics of the PV modules, while Table 2 summarizes the main parameters of the PV system related to the dc-dc boost converter and load, as well as the DE and IC MPPT parameters.

The MPPT techniques were tested considering different operational scenarios as depicted in Fig. 5. In Case 1, represented in Fig. 5a, the PV array is exposed to uniform solar irradiances at $1000W/m^2$. As can be observed, the P-V curve presents only one MPP at 981 W.

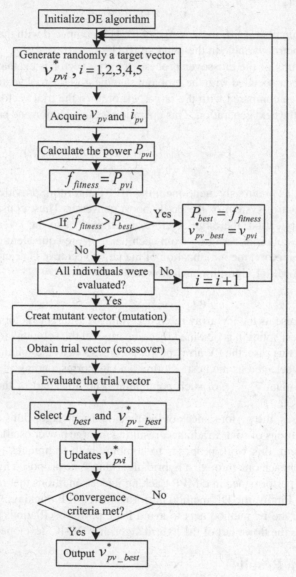

Fig. 3. DE-based MPPT method.

On the other hand, in Case 2, the PV array was subjected to partial shading conditions, as illustrated in Fig. 5b. In this case, the two upper PV modules of the string are subjected to three steps of solar irradiance, resulting in three different patterns of partial shading.

In pattern 1 of partial shading (PS1), from the beginning to 3s of the simulation time, the two upper PV modules are exposed to $900W/m^2$ of solar irradiance. In sequence, in pattern 2 (PS2), from 3 to 5s, $800W/m^2$, and then $1000W/m^2$ for pattern 3 (PS3). The other two modules of the PV array remain unchanged, operating at $300W/m^2$. Moreover, as can be seen from the P-V curves presented in Fig. 5b, the highest power is found in the PS3 with the GMPP located at 478 W. Under PS1 and PS2 conditions, the maximum power is 427 W and 379 W respectively. As expected, the LMPP remains at 310 W for the three patterns of partial shading since solar irradiance has not been changed for the two bottom PV modules.

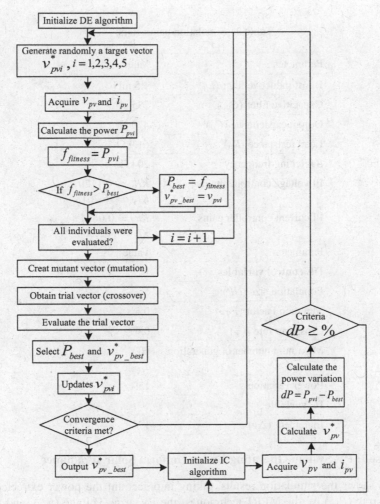

Fig. 4. DE-IC-based MPPT method.

Table 1. Parameters of the photovoltaic (PV) Module at STC.

Parameter	Value
Maximum PV power	245 W
MPP Voltage	30.8 V
MPP Current	7.96 A
Open circuit voltage	37.7 V
Short circuit current	8.25 A

Table 2. Simulation parameters.

Parameter	Value
Boost inductive filter (L_b)	1.5 mH
Capacitive filter (C_{pv})	235 uF
Output capacitance (C_o)	470 uF
Load resistance (R_o)	61.9 Ω
Switching frequency	20 kHz
PI voltage controller gains	$KP_v = 0.1170$ $KI_v = 16.7618$
PI current controller gains	$KP_i = 0.0634$ $KI_i = 302.064$
Parameter	Value
DE control variables	
Population size (NP)	5
Mutation Factor (F)	0.5
Crossover rate (C_r)	0.99
Maximum number of generation (G)	60
Power variation	15%
IC variable	
Increment (Δv)	1 V

4.1   Case 1: PV System Operating Under Uniform Solar Irradiance

Figure 6 shows the simulation results, taking into account the power extracted from the PV array (P_{pv}) by the MPPT techniques, the PV array voltage (v_{pv}), and the PV array current (i_{pv}), under uniform solar irradiance conditions. From Fig. 6, it can be noted that all the implemented MPPT techniques were able to achieve a point close to the GMPP, around 981 W. As can be seen, in the transitory state, the DE-based MPPT and DE-IC-based MPPT algorithms presented high power oscillations due to

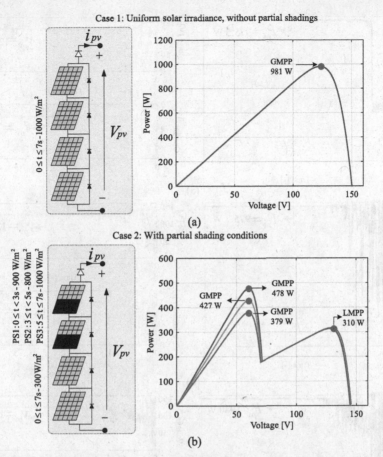

Fig. 5. PV array characteristic curves (P-V): (a) PV array under uniform solar irradiance; (b) PV array under partial shading conditions.

randomness searching. However, under the steady state, the DE algorithm showed small power oscillations compared to IC and DE-IC. Table 3 summarizes the results obtained for Case 1. In terms of convergence time, the IC reached better results when compared with the others, since the MPPTs based on DE took more time in searching space to track the GMPP. On the other hand, the tracking efficiency, calculated from the ratio of the total extracted PV power by the available one, of the hybrid DE-IC resulted in a better performance when compared with the traditional IC and with the DE-based MPPT.

Table 3. Comparison performances among the MPPT techniques based on IC, DE and DE-IC.

Parameter	IC		DE		DE-IC	
	Case 1	Case 2	Case 1	Case 2	Case 1	Case 2
PV power extracted [W]	975.5	307	975.7	463	980	476
Tracking efficiency [%]	99.44	99.03	99.46	96.86	99.89	99.58
Convergence time [s]	0.6	1.8	1.2	2.3	1.8	

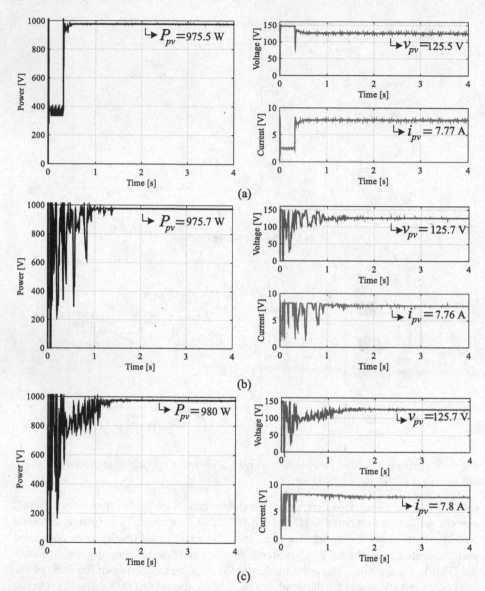

Fig. 6. Simulation results for the MPPT algorithms considering the PV system operating under uniform solar irradiance: (a) IC-based MPPT; (b) DE-based; (c) DE-IC-based MPPT.

4.2 Case 2: PV System Operating Under Partial Shading Conditions

Figure 7 corresponds to the simulation results of Case 2. In this case, three different patterns of partial shading conditions are considered. As can be seen from the results presented in Fig. 7a, the conventional technique based on IC was not able to track the GMPP during the three conditions, demonstrating that its performance was affected when partial shading occurs. On the other hand, as shown in Fig. 7b and Fig. 7c, the MPPT algorithm based on DE as well as the hybrid DE-IC algorithm can sweep the PV characteristic curve exploring all its domains to seek and track the GMPP for different situations.

Considering the partial shading conditions, both MPPTs DE and DE-IC tracked a point close to the GMPP. However, in the hybrid algorithm, the IC method continues the tracking after DE convergence in order to refine the search closer to the ideal operating

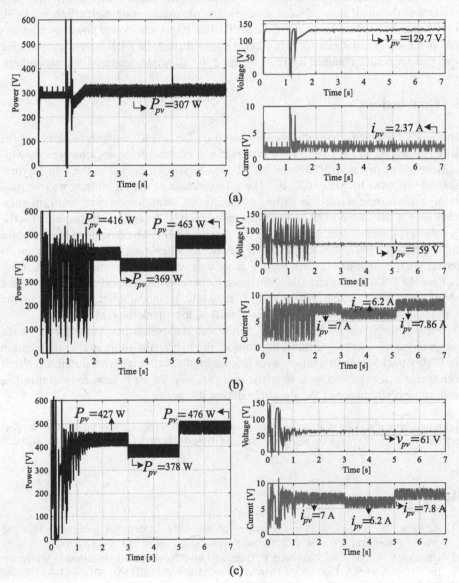

Fig. 7. Simulation results for the MPPT algorithms considering the PV system operating under partial shading conditions: (a) IC-based MPPT; (b) DE-based; (c) DE-IC-based MPPT.

point of the PV array. As a result, the MPPT based on DE-IC extracted more power from the PV array, making it more efficient when compared with the MPPT-DE.

Small variations of solar irradiance tend to represent real situations for operational conditions of a PV system. Nevertheless, the MPPTs based on metaheuristic algorithms require a margin of power variation to restart the random searching and operate properly in transitory conditions. In this work, the power variation was considered 15% of the PV array power. Therefore, small steps of solar irradiance could not be enough to restart the tracking. Hence, it is possible to notice that the algorithm MPPT-DE-IC was able to adapt to the small steps of solar irradiation while maintaining high efficiency in all partial shading patterns. In addition, the MPPT-DE-IC presents lower power oscillations in both transitory and steady states in comparison with the MPPT-DE. Table 3 presents the performance results obtained for PS3 of Case 2, for all implemented MPPT algorithms.

5 Conclusions

This study presented a hybrid algorithm based on DE and IC methods to carry out the MPPT technique in a PV generation system. Such methods were implemented individually, resulting in the MPPT-IC and MPPT-DE algorithms, as well as through a hybrid method proposed by MPPT-DE-IC. The effectiveness of the algorithms was verified through simulation results for different operational conditions. Under uniform solar irradiance (Case 1), the MPPT algorithms based on IC, DE, and DE-IC presented satisfactory performances searching a point close to the GMPP. The efficiency of the hybrid method was superior, due to the ability of the IC adjustments after the DE convergence. On the other hand, when the PV array was subjected to partial shadings (Case 2), the MPPT-IC demonstrated the limitation of conventional methods, tracking only the LMPP and keeping stable at this point. Meanwhile, methods based on meta-heuristic optimization MPPT-DE and MPPT-DE-IC were able to track the GMPP.

Finally, the proposed MPPT-DE-IC presented the overall best performance when compared to the other algorithms. In addition, the hybrid algorithm is able to maintain the GMPP tracked even in small changes in solar irradiance, which is not possible through techniques based only on meta-heuristic optimization. So the losses are minimized as well as the performance of the algorithm makes it superior.

Acknowledgments. This work was supported by FCT national funds, under the national support to R&D units grant, through the reference project UIDB/04436/2020 and UIDP/04436/2020.

References

1. Adefarati, T., Bansal, R. C.: Integration of renewable distributed generators into the distribution system: a review. IET Renew. Power Gener. **10**(7), 873–884 (2016)
2. Dannier, A., Coppola, M., Guerriero, P.: Enhanced MPPT algorithm for multilevel PV inverter. Int. Symp. Power Electron. Electr. Drives Autom. Motion (SPEEDAM) **2018**, 847–852 (2018)
3. Brito, M.A.G., et al.: Evaluation of the main MPPT techniques for photovoltaic applications. IEEE Trans. Ind. Electron. **60**(3), 1156–1167 (2013)

4. Sampaio, L.P., Silva, S.A.O.: Graphic computational platform integrated with an electronic emulator dedicated to photovoltaic systems teaching. IET Power Electron. **10**(14), 1982–1992 (2017)
5. Oliveira, F.M., da Silva, S.A.O., Durand, F.R., Sampaio, L.P., Bacon, V.D., Campanhol, L. B.G.: Grid-tied photovoltaic system based on PSO MPPT technique with active power line conditioning. IET Power Electron. **9**(6), 1180–1191 (2016)
6. Lyden, S., Haque, M.E.: Maximum power point tracking techniques for photovoltaic systems: a comprehensive review and comparative analysis. Renew. Sustain. Energy Rev. **52**, 1504–1518 (2015)
7. Sampaio, L.P., et al.: Comparative analysis of MPPT algorithms bio-inspired by grey wolves employing a feed-forward control loop in a three-phase grid-connected photovoltaic system. IET Renew. Power Gener. **13**(8), 1379–1390 (2019)
8. Podder, A.K., Roy, N.K., Pota, H.R.:MPPT methods for solar PV systems: a critical review based on tracking nature. IET Renew. Power Gener. 13(10), 1615–1632 (2019)
9. Rajabi Moshtaghi, H., Toloie Eshlaghy, A., Motadel, M.R.: A comprehensive review on meta-heuristic algorithms and their classification with novel approach. J. Appl. Res. Industr. Eng. **8**(1), 63–89 (2021)
10. Tey, K.S., Mekhilef, S., Yang, H.T., Chuang, M.K.: A differential evolution based MPPT method for photovoltaic modules under partial shading conditions. Int. J. Photoenergy (2014)
11. Yu, Y., Wang, K., Zhang, T., Wang, Y., Peng, C., Gao, S.: A population diversity-controlled differential evolution for parameter estimation of solar photovoltaic models. Sustain. Energy Technol. Assess. **51**, 101938 (2022)
12. Storn, R., Price, K.: Differential Evolution: a simple and efficient adaptive scheme for global optimization over continuous spaces. ICSI (1995)

Electric Mobility; Power Electronics; Renewable Energy

Development of a Battery Management System for Electric Vehicle's Batteries Reuse

João L. Neto[1] , Marco Silva[1,2] , and Paulo G. Pereirinha[1,2](✉)

[1] Polytechnic of Coimbra, Coimbra Institute of Engineering - ISEC, Rua Pedro Nunes - Quinta da Nora, 3030-199 Coimbra, Portugal
ppereiri@isec.pt
[2] INESC Coimbra, Rua Sílvio Lima, Polo II, 3030-290 Coimbra, Portugal

Abstract. Electric Vehicles (EV) or Plug-in Electric Vehicles (PHEV) batteries can have a second life in other vehicles, in stationary electrical energy storage systems, or in academic or research projects. For this purpose, it is necessary to control and access the battery data through a Battery Management System (BMS), which is often not available in open source, therefore, it is necessary to install and/or develop a new BMS. This article discusses BMS and its features that aim to improve the performance of electric vehicles, optimizing battery capacity during charging and discharging, ensuring the safety and lifetime of a traction battery, promoting sustainable mobility. The process of developing, building, and testing a BMS is presented in this work. It should also be noted that the developed BMS is software configurable, so it can be used with other batteries of the same technology. The battery model under study and the reason to produce a new BMS are briefly reported, as well as the choice of MAX17852, as the data-acquisition Integrated Circuit (IC) used to monitor the battery cells. This work describes the steps taken during the design of all BMS components, including the Printed Circuit Boards (PCBs) design and assembly process, as well as functional tests. It is also addressed the used communication protocols between the BMS elements/components.

Keywords: BMS · Battery Management System Development · Electric Vehicles · PHEV · Traction Battery · Battery Second Life

1 Introduction

Electric energy plays a fundamental role in industrial development, urbanization, and economic advancement, as well as in the quality of life of every human being. Across Europe, countries have been affected by the Covid-19 crisis and the economic recovery plan for these countries emphasizes sustainable mobility, energy efficiency, decarbonization, and the bioeconomy. The transition to clean energy should be highlighted, especially in the integration of electricity from renewable sources [1]. EVs are at the core of the sustainable mobility strategy. Sustainability can be achieved when the energy consumed for the production and operation of EVs is generated by renewable energy sources.

J. L. Afonso et al. (Eds.): SESC 2022, LNICST 502, pp. 95–109, 2023.
https://doi.org/10.1007/978-3-031-33979-0_9

EVs will reduce the environmental impact by being built with long-lasting recharge-able batteries [1] and are much more energy efficient than ICE (internal combustion engine) vehicles. In fact, electric motors benefit from a very high energy efficiency, between 90–95%, when compared to combustion engines, between 20–35%. Electric vehicles do not burn fossil fuels, therefore, EVs motors do not produce direct emissions of pollutant particles or gaseous during their operation [2, 3].

However, with the emergence of electric vehicles, the demand for electricity increases, which can cause imbalances between the energy produced and the energy consumed. Energy must be managed to ensure maximum efficiency from the point of generation to the wheel. Consequently, electric vehicles and all constituent technologies are constantly evolving. Special care must be taken in relation to batteries. Monitoring and proper control of the traction battery is essential in EVs. BMS systems are developed with the aim of protecting and manage batteries parameters' state, as well as their performance. This is responsible for ensuring normal operating conditions, to prolong their useful life and enhance their charge and discharge. These systems are developed with a series of functions, supervising batteries charging and discharging (voltage operation limits, maximum current, and operation temperature), performing cell equalization, analyzing the State of Health (SoH) and the State of Charge (SoC), among other parameters.

There are several battery technologies on the market. However, lithium-ion batteries are currently by far the most used in electric vehicles, due to their notable advantages and significant performance improvements, namely, relatively high energy density and long-life cycles with 80% deep discharge [4].

The development of a BMS presented in this work was motivated by the possibility of reusing HEV (Hybrid Electric Vehicle) and PHEV batteries in second life, and could also be applied in larger capacity batteries, in EVs. In fact, in ISEC electromechanical drives laboratory there are several HEV and PHEV batteries, supplied by PRIO.e company (owner of fuel and EV charging stations), under a collaboration protocol. In particular, the presented case uses a lithium Iron Phosphate battery, $LiFePO_4$, composed of 40 cells, obtained from a Mercedes-Benz PHEV. This battery model was applied to the 350e and 500e ranges. The goal is to use this battery in academic or research applied projects, for the VEIL platform. VEIL is a small EV developed at ISEC targeted for research and teaching. It consisted of a conversion of a small diesel ICE vehicle to EV. It is a LIGIER 162 GL, that weighs about 350 kg, currently equipped with a 400V, 50 Hz, 4 kW, 2860 rpm electric induction motor [5, 6].

With this objective, it was necessary to develop a BMS, starting with the study of which type of BMS to use. Initially, the components and layout of the BMS PCB were addressed, with the objective of creating small size boards, which is a very meticulous process. These PCBs are composed of two layers, and care was taken to separate the power components from the command and communication components to avoid noise or interference.

After this introductory section, this article is organized as follows: Sect. 2 addresses batteries for EVs, namely the battery that is being used in this project and for which the BMS was developed. Section 3 presents battery management systems, what they are for, and what their functions are, highlighting the type of structure used and the reason why it was chosen. In Sect. 4, the processes that the project went through are discussed, describing each stage and the essential elements for the functioning of the BMS, the communication protocols that are used in the project are identified, where they intervene and what is the purpose of each protocol. Section 5 presents the results of some of the tests developed and, finally, Sect. 6 ends this work with conclusions.

2 Batteries for EVs

In EVs, rechargeable batteries (also called secondary) are used exclusively. A traction battery normally is made of several modules, each consisting of cell sets, which can be combined in series and/or parallel, in order to obtain the desired voltage, current and capacity [7].

For the project described in this work, a $LiFePO_4$ battery was used due to its availability and state of conservation. Lithium-ion batteries have established themselves as the reference technology in the world market for electric vehicles. These batteries are designed as a set of individual cells, which linked together form a battery, being monitored by a dedicated electronic circuit. The number of cells, the size of each cell and the way they are arranged determine the voltage supplied by the battery and its capacity, that is, the amount of electric energy that can be stored [8].

The main reason for the large-scale success of lithium-ion batteries is essentially the storage density that the technology allows. This concept of density refers to the relationship between storage capacity and volume or weight. These values can be compared, with a lithium-ion battery offering a density about ten times more than a lead-acid battery.

In Fig. 1 it is possible to visualize the battery used in this project, composed of 40 prismatic cells (2 strings of 20 cells in series). Usually, in this type of cells, aluminum or steel is used as casing material of the lithium-ion cells, guaranteeing structural stability, mechanical strength, and protection against moisture. Prismatic cells allow the space packed to be more efficiently packed than with cylindrical cells due to their shape. The use of prismatic cells allows constraining and retaining cells within their structure, with potentially higher energy density, but requires a complex module structure. The large surface area becomes beneficial due to thermal management. It is currently the most used cell format in electric vehicles [9, 10].

The thermal stability that lithium-ion batteries offer (depending on the used chemistry) must be considered to guaranty the needed safety. They enable fast charging, as well as reducing the use of raw materials, synthetic processes, and the use of low toxicity materials. These batteries also have functional issues, for example, they cannot be fully discharged because the battery can be irreversibly damaged, in case of cells' unbalance; therefore, it is common to have a protection circuit connected to the battery to keep the voltage and current within the limits established by the manufacturer. The charge of these batteries must be monitored, as they are not very tolerant to overloads or overdischarges. $LiFePO_4$ batteries, as mentioned in Table 1, are an interesting option within the lithium-ion batteries. They offer good electrochemical performance with low resistance, high rated current, good thermal stability, long life cycles and increased safety [3, 7]. These batteries present some self-discharge rate, which can cause imbalances with

Fig. 1. LiFePO4 battery, used in the project

aging, requiring more attention and the use of more effective monitoring systems. This battery is not tolerant to humidity, drastically reducing its longevity [8, 10].

Table 1. Main characteristics of the used battery

Specifications	Lithium-Iron Phosphate Battery (LiFePO$_4$)
Energy (kWh)	2.9 kWh
Min/Max Cell voltage (V)	2 V/3.65 V
Nominal module voltage (V)	2x66 V
Current (Ah)	22,8 Ah
Number Cells in Series	2x20S
Anode / Cathode	Graphite / LiFePO$_4$

3 Battery Management System

The EV's battery operating voltage is variable, and the battery capacity depends on the system power and autonomy. To obtain the voltage and power required for the vehicle, it is necessary to apply cells interconnected in series and/or parallel, and there may be a voltage imbalance between them, causing a decrease in the capacity and in the useful life of the vehicle. Battery [3, 11].

The battery operation management is carried out by the BMS, which monitor and control the cells status of the battery or a batteries bank. Its main objectives are to protect the cells and the battery against damage, extend the life of the batteries, keep the battery in a working state in order to supply the requested requirements and communicate with a higher-level system, usually the Vehicle Control Unit (VCU). For that, the BMS is an electronic system that controls the performance of individual cells, with the aim of avoiding: overcharges, excessively deep discharges, exceeding the maximum and minimum limits of cell voltages, high temperatures, and short circuits. When one of these previously discussed limits falls within outside the programmed parameters range, the battery must be removed from operation, preventing the occurrence of accidents or even failures with greater damage.

In terms of the physical structure of the BMS, these depend on the number of cells used and the requirements of the system. BMS architectures can be classified as Centralized (each cell is connected to one unique central system), Modular (BMS is divided into multiple modules), Master-Slave (similar to modular architecture but the data processing is done in additional master module) and Distributed (each cell has its own data acquisition board). The main differences of this architectures can be verified at [12].

4 BMS Development Case Study

The battery being used for this study already contained a proprietary BMS but there was no access to its operation protocol, so it was necessary to install a new BMS. Initially, the market was researched for which BMS could satisfy the case study. Commercial BMS were not chosen because many of them do not offer an open-source solution neither allow access to all the intended parameters. Thus, it was decided to use a dedicated data acquisition system integrated circuit and create the entire BMS structure from scratch.

During this search, the integrated circuits that stood out for the proposed needs are listed in Table 2, presenting their main characteristics.

Table 2. Data acquisition ICs analyzed for the BMS project

Integrated	BQ76952	Max17852	LTC6813
N° Cells	16	14	18
HV Tolerance	85 V	80 V	75 V
Balancing up to	100 mA	650 mA	200 mA
cell accuracy worst case	± 5 mV	± 4.5 mV	± 4.2 mV

The Max17852 was chosen, mainly for its greater balancing capacity and for verifying that Maxim Integrated has a development Kit, the Max17852 EV Kit, which allows to demonstrate the resources and capabilities of the Max17852. This EV kit, through jumpers and switches, makes possible to carry out some configurations according to the user's needs. In this way, the Max17852 EV Kit served as a starting point for the PCB board design around the analog front end IC.

The Master-Slave model was chosen, due to its characteristics. As shown below in Fig. 2 it is possible to verify how this typology is structured.

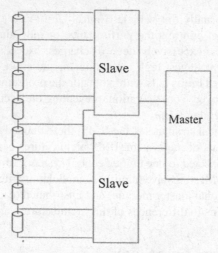

Fig. 2. Example of BMS typology with Master-Slave structure [13].

In the Master-Slave structure, there are two different types of BMS modules, Master and Slave. The Master-Slave structure is similar to a modular system; it uses several identical modules (slaves), in the developed system each module measures the voltage of 10 cells. However, the master is different from the modules and does not measure voltages, it only handles computing and communications. This structure is recommended for applications with a high number of cells; in the case of the Max17852, up to 32 devices can be daisy-chained to manage 448 cells and monitor 128 temperatures. This structure is ideal for situations where it is predictable or desired to increase the number of cells (or modules). Although it is the model that has the highest implementation cost, it is the one that makes it easier to expand the number of cells [11].

In a first analysis, the crucial aspects for the functioning of the BMS were verified, such as the Universal Asynchronous Receiver Transmitter (UART) communication mode. For robust communications, the system uses Maxim's battery-management UART protocol, is optimized to support a reduced feature set of internal diagnostics and rapid-alert communication through both embedded communication and hardware-alert interfaces to support ASIL-D and FMEA requirements.

These can be the Battery-Management UART Protocol or SPI, Fig. 3, depending on the hardware configurations, but they cannot be dynamically changed: the UARTSEL pin allows the configuration of this interface.

In order to maximize the integrity of communications, the battery-management UART protocol uses several features: all transmitted data bytes are Manchester-encoded, (G.E. Thomas convention), every transmitted character contains 12 bits, which include a start bit, a parity bit, and two stop bits, read/write packets contain a CRC-8 Packet-Error Checking (PEC) byte, each packet is framed by a preamble character and stop character and read packets contains a data-check byte for verifying the integrity of the transmission [14].

In this project the Single UART Interface with External Loopback is used and it is possible to check all the settings for the UART interface at [14] pp. 58. This UART protocol allows capacitive communication-port isolation, up to 2 Mbps baud rate (auto-detect) and Packet-Error Checking (PEC).

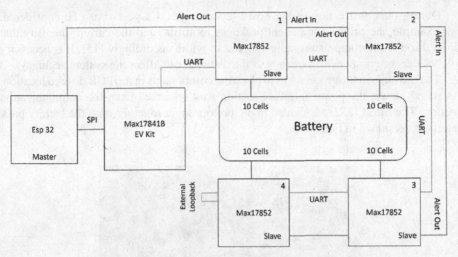

Fig. 3. Developed BMS block diagram.

The UART receiver has a wide common-mode input range to tolerate harsh EMC (Electromagnetic compatibility) ([14] pp. 132). MAX17852 is a high voltage data acquisition system, Automotive Safety Integrity Level D (ASIL D), with 14 voltage measuring channels and integrated current sensing amplifier.

Having defined the BMS structure, the schematic was developed, as can be seen in Fig. 4. To develop the PCB boards schematic and layout, based on the Max17852 EV Kit, the Autodesk Eagle software [15] was used.

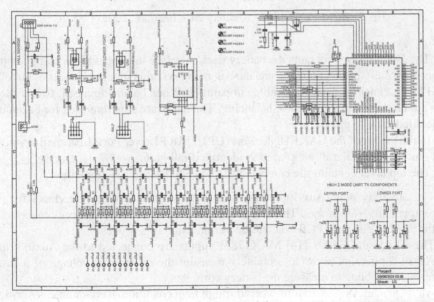

Fig. 4. PCB schematic.

During the construction of the board layout, several aspects must be considered. For example, the proper component packages footprint, and the current intensity that flows through the components, adjusting tracks width accordingly [15]. It is necessary to consider the components position, as the distance can affect the system accuracy.

The next step in the process was to place the components in the PCB desired location. As stated above, the power interface section was separated from the communication section. The Max17852 was placed in the bottom layer together with the battery pack interface, as shown in Fig. 5.

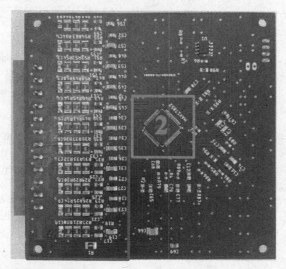

Fig. 5. Bottom Layer PCB: 1-Battery Pack Interface, 2-Max17852IC.

The Bottom layer contains the battery pack interface that includes as main components the battery connection plug and the balancing resistors mounted in sets of three 22 Ω (1210 package) resistors assembled in parallel. When balancing a cell, two of these sets are used, performing passive balancing. The hardware structure used for balancing is detailed at ([14] pp. 202).

In the top layer, the UART Upper Port (UP), UART Lower Port (LP), auxiliary ports and the in and out alarms are placed as identified in Fig. 6.

The top layer contains the components for the following functionalities:

- The auxiliary pins (Aux Input and Aux Output) provide direct interfaces for the temperature NTC probes. This is accomplished by 10 kΩ NTC sensors connected to the THRM pin, each PCB board allows connection of 3 probes.
- The CSAP and CSAN [14] MAX17852 inputs are connected to the Auxin 4 and Auxin 5 pins that allow to accurately measure the differential voltage of a shunt resistor, enabling to measure the battery current.
- Alert Out and Alert In perform alerts through fault condition. It communicates critical safety failures, whether these are: voltage measurements, temperature measurements, interface communication failures, calibration, and other hardware diagnostics [14].

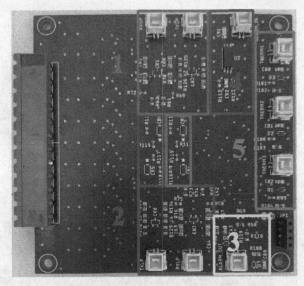

Fig. 6. Top Layer PCB: 1-UART UP, 2-UART LP, 3-Alert Out LP, 4-Alert In UP, 5-Aux Input, Aux Output, Current Sensor Amplifier interface (CSA, at JP1- right bottom).

- The UART LP and UART UP communication ports are identified as the upper port (RXUP/TXUP) and the lower port (RXLP/TXLP), referring to the MAX17852 device on the PCB. Each UART port includes a differential transmitter and a differential receiver. Communication data received at the lower receiver (RXL) is relayed via the upper transmitter (TXU) to the next PCB board, daisy-chained. Communication received at the upper receiver (RXU) is relayed through the lower transmitter (TXL) and down the chain.

Once the layout of the PCB boards was finished, their external production was requested. While the boards were being produced, the necessary components were requested to carry out the assembly. Each board is composed of 202 components.

The association of the PCB boards aimed to manage the 40 cells of the LiFePO$_4$ battery. For this purpose, 4 PCB boards were developed, therefore each board allows monitoring 10 cells. In the future, a PCB will be developed to support the ESP32 microcontroller, which will include the Max17841B, to remove the Max17841 EV-KIT used only for development. In Fig. 7, it is possible to visualize the assembly of the 4 boards, after components soldering, through hot air, at ISEC laboratory.

Fig. 7. - Four BMS PCBs mounted on a first battery test.

In Fig. 8 the fundamental process phases for carrying out the project are described, and it is currently in the experimental testing phase.

As mentioned above, there are many aspects to consider when designing a printed circuit board. The length and width of the tracks are important when the layout is made, considering the applied voltage and current. Tracks can be on inner or outer layers, but in this case, there are only tracks on the outer layers. The fact that there are only tracks in the outer layers allows them to have smaller widths than in the inner layers, due to heat dissipation. In Battery pack interface area (Fig. 5), a current of approximately 1A was considered (balancing currents will be less than 350 mA), hence for balancing was selected a track width of 0.508 mm, and in the remaining board, for control/communications it was considered 0.254 mm. All calculations were performed to have a track temperature raise below 5°C at a room temperature of 25 °C. The PCB board size is 99x97x1.6 (mm). An online tool can be of great importance to quickly evaluate the proper track width to use regarding the temperature rise and layer thickness [16].

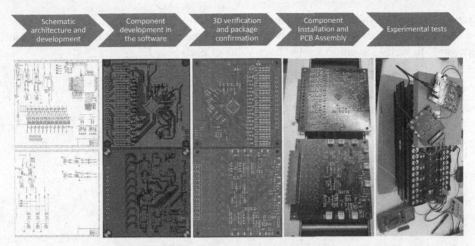

Fig. 8. Processes developed during the project.

After all the PCBs were connected in series, they must be connected to the EV VCU. To manage the BMS connection to the EV, an ESP32 microcontroller can be used to implement an open-source interface protocol. One advantage of this microcontroller is that it offers Bluetooth and Wi-Fi connectivity. This enables, for example, to create an Android BMS management APP.

Max17852 IC boards use the battery-management UART Protocol to interconnect, so the ESP32 must use Max17841B through SPI as a transceiver to the UART interface. It is also possible for the daisy-chained BMS boards to be connected through a MAX17841B EV KIT [18] with a Windows PC application, for example, using the Max17853 Evaluation Kit Software [17].

For greater security, the MAX17852 UART has Manchester encryption, and it was decided to purchase the MAX17841B EV KIT [18] for the decoding interface to the ESP microcontroller [14]. The chosen Max17852 allows two types of communication protocols to control the data acquisition. These can be the UART protocol or SPI, depending on the hardware configurations, but they cannot be dynamically changed: the UARTSEL pin ([14] pp. 176) allows the configuration of this interface.

5   Trials and Tests

Initially, to be able to carry out all the tests safely, mainly to confirm the normal functioning of the BMS boards after assembly, the tests were carried out without a battery. In this case, ten 2 kΩ resistors were installed in series, creating a voltage divider, to replace a battery, with the use of a power supply. To apply the equivalent voltages, resistors were installed between cells C0 to C10 inputs terminals, which in turn allow the voltage measurement reading of Max17852 [14]. Communications and cell reading essays were performed. Initially, the readings obtained were made using the Max17853 Evolution Kit software [17]–[19]. Figure 9 shows tests being carried out in real-time, obtaining the voltage values of the 40 cells. Aux In 2 (AIN2 Fig. 9) shows the temperature value of four NTC sensors (one for each board). The temperature is scaled in volts. It is also possible to verify the group total voltage value of each board.

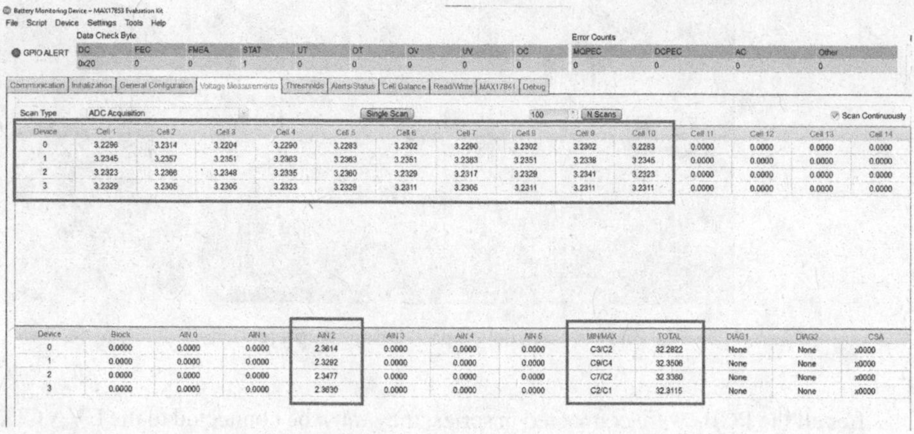

Fig. 9. Real-time reading of 10 battery cells through the Max17853 EV Kit software [14].

With tests evolution, the acquisition of cell values, temperature values and low and high voltage alarms were tested. Next, ESP-32 was used with C programming, also reading the parameters discussed above, and the balancing strategy techniques are being evaluated. Table 3 shows voltage and temperature values obtained after reading the 40 cells, using the setup presented in Fig. 7, being possible to verify through the photos at the bottom of the table the confirmation of the values using a high accuracy voltage meter from BK Precision (around 1 mV difference).

During the tests carried out, it was possible to analyze the behavior of the IC board in relation to possible hot spots. This test makes it possible to analyze if any component is overheating as hot spots may occur, for example, due to a bad soldering or a damaged component. After several hours of operation, the device temperature remained within the same values. In Fig. 10 it is possible to verify, through a photograph taken by a thermographic camera, the place where the temperature is highest, which in this case is where the Max17852 is placed, but well within the values recommended by the manufacturer [14].

Table 3. Data acquisition test on a serial monitor application.

DEVICE: 1	DEVICE: 2	DEVICE: 3	DEVICE: 4
Cell 1: 3.224V	Cell 1: 3.227V	Cell 1: 3.228V	Cell 1: 3.224V
Cell 2: 3.224V	Cell 2: 3.231V	Cell 2: 3.230V	Cell 2: 3.226V
Cell 3: 3.226V	Cell 3: 3.230V	Cell 3: 3.229V	Cell 3: 3.213V
Cell 4: 3.225V	Cell 4: 3.229V	Cell 4: 3.229V	Cell 4: 3.224V
Cell 5: 3.228V	Cell 5: 3.231V	Cell 5: 3.230V	Cell 5: 3.225V
Cell 6: 3.225V	Cell 6: 3.230V	Cell 6: 3.228V	Cell 6: 3.225V
Cell 7: 3.227V	Cell 7: 3.229V	Cell 7: 3.228V	Cell 7: 3.225V
Cell 8: 3.225V	Cell 8: 3.229V	Cell 8: 3.230V	Cell 8: 3.225V
Cell 9: 3.226V	Cell 9: 3.229V	Cell 9: 3.229V	Cell 9: 3.226V
Cell 10: 3.221V	Cell 10: 3.226V	Cell 10: 3.226V	Cell 10: 3.223V
Min / Max Cell Voltages: C10 / C5	Min / Max Cell Voltages: C10 / C2	Min / Max Cell Voltages: C10 / C5	Min / Max Cell Voltages: C3 / C2
Block Voltage: 32.282V	Block Voltage: 32.314V	Block Voltage: 32.321V	Block Voltage: 32.258V
Temperature Cell: 24.772°C	Temperature Cell: 24.534°C	Temperature Cell: 24.813°C	Temperature Cell: 24.402°C
BK PRECISION 5491B 50000 Count Multimeter 3225c̄ ꞁ DC	*Device 1 Cell 1*	BK PRECISION 5491B 50000 Count Multimeter 32249 ꞁ DC	*Device 1 Cell 2*

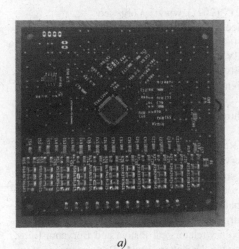
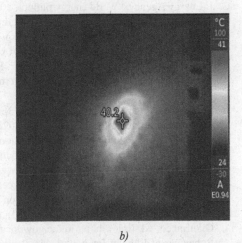

a)   *b)*

Fig. 10. a) Board assembly, b) Thermography performed on the IC board.

6 Conclusion

In this article the development of a BMS for a LiFePO$_4$ battery was presented. The Data Acquisition System IC, MAX17852, is showing to be a good option for the battery reuse requirement. The developed PCB board includes all the control and monitoring configurations necessary for this battery technology.

This developed BMS is intended to be part of an Open-Source system and to allow working with other batteries of the same typology. The balancing system is currently being studied and carried out to integrate with the remaining experimental tests. The system can also be used to develop algorithms for SoC, SoH and other academic and research projects.

Acknowledgements. This work was partially supported by FCT – Portuguese Foundation for Science and Technology under INESC Coimbra (DEEC, Coimbra, Portugal) project UIDB/00308/2020.

The authors would also like to thank Prio Energy (www.prio.pt/pt/) for the partnership in this project, providing the used LiFePO$_4$ battery, and to Maxim Integrated (www.maximintegrated.com/en) for providing Max17852 samples for the development of the PCB boards.

References

1. I. Energy Agency, "Electric and plug-in hybrid vehicle roadmap" (2009). www.iea.org/roadmaps
2. I. Energy Agency, "World energy outlook 2021" (2021). www.iea.org/weo
3. Pereirinha, P.G.: Electric vehicles, in reference module in materials science and materials engineering. Elsevier (2022). https://doi.org/10.1016/B978-0-12-821204-2.00112-4
4. Consulting, T.B.: Battery Packs of Modern xEVs - Report Extract (2019)
5. Pereirinha, P.G., Trovao, J.P., Marques, L., Silva, M., Silvestre, J., Santos, F.: Advances in the electric vehicle project-VEIL used as a modular platform for research and education Oct (2009)
6. Pereirinha, P. et al.: VEIL Project Jul. (2013). https://www.isec.pt/pt/instituto/departamentos/dee/veil/index_en.htm. Accessed 10 Jan 2022
7. Matthey, J.: Guide to Batteries ur 3rd Edition Re-print (2017)
8. Buchmann, I.: Battery University. https://batteryuniversity.com/ Accessed 12 Jul 2022
9. SDI, S.: Samsung SDI Product. https://www.samsungsdi.com/automotive-battery/products/prismatic-lithium-ion-battery-cell.html Accessed 25 Jan 2022
10. Chen, T., et al.: Applications of lithium-ion batteries in grid-scale energy storage systems. Trans. Tianjin Univ. **26**(3), 208–217 (2020). https://doi.org/10.1007/s12209-020-00236-w
11. Gianfranco. ed. (role). http://id.loc.gov/vocabulary/relators/edt Pistoia and Boryann, Liaw, Behaviour of Lithium-Ion batteries in electric vehicles battery health, Performance, Safety, and Cost, 1st ed. 2018 (2018). http://lib.ugent.be/catalog/ebk01:3840000000347744
12. Pistoia, G.: Electric and Hybrid Vehicles, 1^a. (2010)
13. Andrea, D.: Battery management systems for large lithium-ion battery packs (2010)
14. M. Integrated, MAX 17852 - 14-Channel High-Voltage, ASIL D,Data-Acquisition System with Integrated Current-Sense. Dec. (2020). www.maximintegrated.com
15. Autodesk Inc., "Eagle Software," 2022. autodesk.com/products/eagle/overview?term=1-YEAR&tab=subscription#what-is-eagle-. Accessed 21 Oct 2021

16. Suppanz, B.: 4pcb.com (2018). https://www.4pcb.com/trace-width-calculator.html. Accessed 20 Oct 2022
17. Maxim Integrated, How to Measure Voltage, Current and Temperature of a Battery Pack Using the MAXREFDES1277, Part 1, (Jul. 30, 2021). Accessed 20 Oct 2022. https://www.youtube.com/watch?v=09CIWosaFN8
18. M. Integrated: MAX17841B Evaluation Kit/General Description (2018). www.maximintegrated.com
19. M. Integrated: MAX17852 Evaluation Kit/General Description (2020). www.maximintegrated.com

DC-DC Power Converter for High Power Solar Photovoltaic System

João P. D. Miranda[1]($\boxtimes$), Duarte M. N. Rodrigues[1]($\boxtimes$), Luis A. M. Barros[1,2], and J. G. Pinto[1,2]

[1] Department of Industrial Electronics, University of Minho, Guimarães, Portugal
{pg47332,pg47158}@alunos.uminho.pt
[2] ALGORITMI Centre/LASI–University of Minho, Guimarães, Portugal

Abstract. Worldwide there is an enormous dependence on fossil fuels to produce electricity. Burning fossil fuels results in CO_2 emission into the atmosphere, causing a negative environmental impact. In order to mitigate these problems, there is a need to integrate renewable energy sources into the power grid, namely solar photovoltaic (PV) energy. Power electronics converter solutions for solar PV module interface are vast and have advantages and disadvantages depending on the purpose. In addition, when the purpose is efficiency, it is important to consider the choice of the most appropriate power semiconductors.

This paper presents a study, sizing, and development of a DC-DC power converter for high-power solar PV applications. In this study, a DC-DC boost interleaved power converter with two arms controlled by an incremental conductance Maximum Power Point Tracking (MPPT) control algorithm is proposed. The MPPT is combined with a Proportional-Integral (PI) controller for individual control of the current on each arm and was applied to extract the maximum power available at the solar PV module for different solar radiation and temperature conditions. The digital control system was implemented in a TMS320F28335 microcontroller from Texas Instruments.

Keywords: DC-DC boost interleaved converter · Incremental conductance MPPT · PI controller · Renewable Energies · Solar photovoltaic system

1 Introduction

Renewable energy sources play a key role in the *Roadmap for Carbon Neutrality 2050* [1]. This roadmap establishes, in a sustained way, the path to achieving carbon neutrality in 2050, defining the main guidelines and identifying the cost-effective options to achieve the intended result in different socio-economic development scenarios. Achieving carbon neutrality implies, together with other measures, the total decarbonization of the electro-producing system. At the end of 2021, Portugal closed its last coal-based power plant in operation, the Pego thermoelectric plant [2]. It is also committed to achieving a target of 80% of the energy produced from renewable energy. However, according to ADENE, this target can be brought forward to 2025 [3].

© ICST Institute for Computer Sciences, Social Informatics and Telecommunications Engineering 2023
Published by Springer Nature Switzerland AG 2023. All Rights Reserved
J. L. Afonso et al. (Eds.): SESC 2022, LNICST 502, pp. 110–125, 2023.
https://doi.org/10.1007/978-3-031-33979-0_10

Solar photovoltaic (PV) modules produce electricity from solar energy. They are composed of a combination of PV cells associated in series and/or parallel to obtain higher power units, as presented in [4]. Analyzing the electrical model of a solar PV cell, it is possible to verify that it has a current source operating mode. Therefore, It the integration of a power electronics converter, with constant input current, that guarantees a continuous extraction of the energy of the solar PV module, allows greater efficiency of the system [5].

This work presents a study on multi-string solar PV systems configurations, DC-DC boost interleaved converter, Incremental Conductance (IC), and proportional-integral (PI) algorithms with experimental validation. This project aims to contribute to the design and implementation of a power converter solution capable of integrating a high-power solar PV system. This document is organized into five sections, as follows: Sect. 1 introduces the subject; Sect. 2 describes the implemented power converter; Sect. 3 presents the simulations on the number of arms, switching frequency, and control circuit; Sect. 4 shows the experimental validations and in Sect. 5, the main conclusions are presented.

2 Proposed Converter

2.1 Solar PV System Configurations and Hardware Components

Solar PV systems can be configured in a variety of ways, namely centralized, string and ac-module configurations [6]. For high-power applications multi-string configuration stands out. The multi-string structure described in Fig. 1 has several strings of solar PV modules connected in series, interfaced with their DC-DC power converter to a common dc-ac power converter. This configuration uses only one dc-ac power converter, a lower cost, and greater simplicity and flexibility when compared to other configurations while allowing the application of the Maximum Power Point Tracking (MPPT) control algorithm individually.

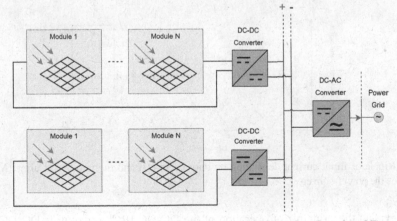

Fig. 1. Solar PV system based on multi-string configuration (based on [6]).

A very important aspect in the design of a power converter is related to the hardware to be used, namely the power semiconductors. Newer technologies such as silicon carbide (SiC) and gallium nitridet (GaN) offer advantages compared to other technologies such as insulated-gate bipolar transistor (IGBT), especially for high-power applications, highlighting smaller losses, better conductivity, and operation at higher temperatures, which results in more compact power converters [7]. Since both technologies serve the purpose of the application and SiC is presently more accessible than GaN, this technology is proposed in the current work [8].

2.2 DC-DC Interleaved Boost Converter

In all studied topologies such as conventional boost [9], cascaded boost [10], switched-capacitor boost [11], switched-inductor boost [12], the DC-DC interleaved boost converter (IBC) topology presents several advantages for high-power applications. In this topology, the output of the power converters is associated in parallel, which allows for achieving higher power values than when used separately.

Among the advantages of this topology, the smallest ripple of the input current and the output voltage stand out [13]. The current in each arm also has a lower value, which implies lower ohmic losses in the inductances, with greater efficiency and lower cost (due to a lower use of copper). When the current ripple is small, the input power becomes practically constant allowing for continuous energy extraction from solar PV modules.

In Eq. (1), the operation duty cycle (D) is represented as a function of the ratio of the input voltage (V_i) to the output voltage (V_o). On the other hand, Fig. 2 compares the ripple values of the current to different arm numbers (N) and semiconductor operation D. Thus, is possible to conclude that the use of a two-arm IBC allows for halving the maximum ripple of the input current when compared to the use of only one arm [13].

$$D = 1 - \frac{V_i}{V_o} \tag{1}$$

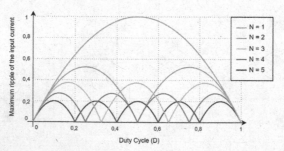

Fig. 2. Ripple of input current depending on duty cycle (D) and the number of arms (N) that composes the power converter.

To explain the principle of operation of the DC-DC IBC, a two-arms DC-DC IBC was used, as shown in Fig. 3. It consists of two conventional boost power converters connected in parallel to operate alternately. The inductor L_1, the metal-oxide-semiconductor filed-effect transistor (MOSFET) S_1, and the diode D_1 form the first converter, while the inductor L_2, the MOSFET S_2, and the diode D_2 form the second converter. Each MOSFET device presents an internal free-wheeling diode. The two-arm DC-DC IBC shares the same capacitor, C_1, at the output. The phase-shift angle of the MOSFET pulse width modulation (PWM) signal is given by 360°/N, being N the number of arms of the power converter. In the case of two-arm DC-DC IBC, the PWM signals of the MOSFET S_1 lags the PWM signal of MOSFET S_2 by 180°. In turn, the number of MOSFET in simultaneous conduction depends on the value of D.

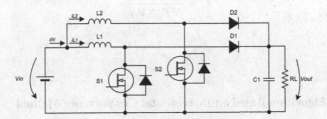

Fig. 3. Electrical schematic of the DC-DC IBC with two arms.

Figure 4 presents the operation principle of the power converter for two operation modes: (i) Fig. 4 (a) for $D < 0.5$; (ii) and Fig. 4 (b) for D values ≥ 0.5. Considering the first condition, MOSFET never conducts at the same time. To study the behavior of the converter in this region, and consider the continuous conduction mode, it is possible to divide the operation into four stages [14]. Assuming that the parameters of the two converters are identical, a merely illustrative example of the theoretical waveforms of MOSFET control and currents in the inductors is shown in Fig. 4.

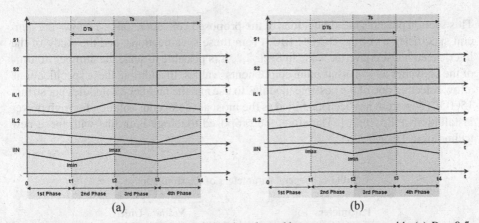

Fig. 4. Theoretical waveforms of the DC-DC interleaved boost converter type with: (a) $D < 0.5$; (b) $D \geq 0.5$.

For this topology to operate within the expected specifications, it is necessary to correctly size the components. If the inductors have similar characteristics and the operation of the converter in CCM, their value can be calculated according to Eq. (2), where V_{in} is the converter input voltage, D is the duty cycle, N is the number of arms of the converter, f_s is the switching frequency and $\Delta I_{L1, L2}$ is the current ripple on the respective inductor. Based on Eq. (3) it is possible to determine the value of the capacitor, being necessary to consider the value of the output current, $Iout$, which can be obtained using Eq. (4) [14].

$$L_1 = L_2 = \frac{V_{in}D}{Nf_s \Delta I_{L1,L2}} \tag{2}$$

$$C = \frac{I_{Out}D}{Nf_s \Delta V_{Out}} \tag{3}$$

$$\frac{I_{out}}{I_{in}} = 1 - D \tag{4}$$

2.3 MPPT Algorithm Based on Incremental Conductance Method

Among the various algorithms, there are two that stand out among the others: Perturbation and Observation (P&O) and Incremental Conductance (IC) [15]. Based on the bibliographic study, it is possible to conclude that both methods present a simple algorithm with good performance regardless of the operating conditions. However, the IC method has an additional advantage in the fact that voltage remains constant as soon as the maximum power point (MPP) is reached and reacts to greater temperature and radiation variations [16]. Authors present in [17] a c-code of the IC MPPT control algorithm integrated into a microinverter.

3 Simulation Results

This section presents the simulations of the proposed converter. Table 1 shows the general specifications of the DC-DC IBC. From these specifications, and the study of the interleaved boost converter made in Sect. 2.2, it is possible to scale the number of arms of the converter as well as its main components' values. In addition, these specifications allow selecting one of the possible modules to use and the number of modules per string. 1500 V PV system has been identified as the most advantageous solution for high power installations [18, 19, 20]. Therefore, the proposed topology is in line with these new technological trends.

Table 1. General parameters of the simulations.

Parameter	Value	Unit
Nominal Input Voltage (V_{Nin})	1200	V
Open Circuit Input Voltage (V_{OCin})	1500	V

(continued)

Table 1. (*continued*)

Parameter	Value	Unit
Input Current (I_{in})	12	A
DC Bus Output Voltage (V_{out})	2000	V
Input Current Ripple (ΔI_{in})	10	%
Output Voltage Ripple (ΔV_{in})	1	%

Replacing the DC-DC IBC input and output voltage values in Eq. (4), a D of 40% is obtained. Components such as inductors and MOSFET devices can only be selected after determining the number of arms of the DC-DC IBC since the current that crosses them is directly related to this parameter.

3.1 Study on the Number of Arms

As stated in Sect. 2.2, the number of arms influences the input current ripple. Simulations were then performed, with a switching frequency (f_s) of 40 kHz, for different numbers of arms. Table 2 shows the values of the inductors and capacitors calculated based on Eqs. (2) and (3), respectively, for the different numbers of arms and specifications of Table 1. Analyzing the data, it is possible to conclude that for the same operating conditions the greater the number of arms, the lower the value of the passive components. The simulation results for one, two, three, and five arms are present in Fig. 5.

Table 2. Capacitor and inductor values to a different number of arms.

Number of Arms	L (mH)	C (μF)
1	10	3.6
2	5	1.8
3	3.3	0.9
5	2	0.72

As can be seen in Fig. 5 for a $D = 0.4$ case, the five-arm interleaved converter is the one with the smallest input current ripple, ($I \Delta_{in}$). Topologies with two and three arms have very similar and better results than the one-arm converter. It is important to note that a larger number of arms implies a higher failure probability as well as a higher implementation cost. However, a larger number of arms allows for greater redundancy. That is, in the event of a one-arm failure, if the converter does not have any additional arms, the system may operate in excess load or even fail to function. Given all these factors, one chose to develop a two arm IBC. The two arm converter solution allows for validation of the concept of interleaved without major implementation costs.

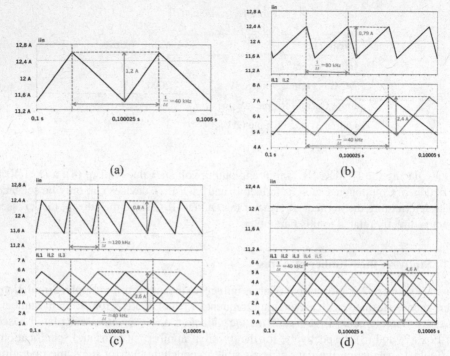

Fig. 5. Simulation results for different arm numbers, $fs = 40$ kHz: (a) 1 arm; (b) 2 arms; (c) 3 arms; (d) 5 arms.

3.2 Study on the Switching Frequency

From Table 1 is known that the power converter has a maximum input current of 12 A and an output voltage of 2000 V. Once established the use a two-arm IBC power converter it is possible to select the value of the inductors and power semiconductors, SiC in this particular case. The main criterion for selecting the value of the inductor and the frequency to be used is the value of the losses in the inductors and SiC. In a DC-DC IBC with a 10% ripple, the inductor losses (P_L) do not vary significantly with frequency. The main cause for losses is the winding internal dc resistance, R_{DC}. It is possible to calculate the inductor power losses using Eq. (5), where I is the root mean square value of the current that crosses the inductor, in this case as the current is almost constant there is no difference between rms and dc values. Switching and conduction losses in SiC MOSFET can be estimated using the PSIM tool which allows the selected semiconductor model to be inserted [21].

$$P_L = R_{DC}I^2(W) \tag{5}$$

Each inductor must be able to support the maximum current in each arm, which is half of the input current, i.e., 6 A. Thus, a set of 10 A high-frequency "197 DC series" inductors from Hammond Manufacturing [22] was selected, where the main characteristics are presented in Table 3. Nevertheless, the table also shows the frequency and output capacitor values calculated based on Eqs. (2) and (3), respectively, for the different values of the inductors.

Table 3. Hammond Manufacturing series 10 A dc inductors.

L (mH)	DC Resistance (mΩ)	P_L (W)	Frequency (kHz)	C (μF)
1	232	8.352	200	1.8
3.5	293	10.548	57.1	1.03
7.5	403	14.508	26.7	0.72

Table 4. Calculation of the total power losses concerning the inductance and switching frequency.

L (mH)	Frequency (kHz)	P_L (W)	$P_{switching}$ (W)	$P_{conduction}$ (W)	Total Losses (W)
1	200	8.352	226.9	1.97	237.2
3.5	57.1	10.548	60.05	1.71	72.31
7.5	26.7	14.508	28.46	1.75	42.72

Similarly, each SiC MOSFET will also have to conduct a current of 6 A and withstand a voltage equal to the dc-link voltage, 2000 V. It was thus decided to use the G2R120MT33J SiC from GeneSic [23], capable of supporting 3300 V and conducting 33 A.

Table 5 contains the values obtained in the simulation of conduction and switching SiC losses, inductor losses, and total losses, corresponding to the sum of the last three. Since the current ripple obtained for the three cases is virtually equal, the criterion for selecting f_s and the inductor to be used is related to the total losses of the circuit. Analyzing the results can be concluded that the lower losses occur for the inductor with 7.5 mH and a switching frequency of 26.7 kHz.

3.3 Control Circuit

In a two-arm IBC, the real value of each arm inductor may be slightly different. Since the current must divide into each arm in a balanced way, two proportional-integral (PI) controllers are used to regulate the current in each arm as balanced as possible.

3.4 PSIM Solar PV Physical Model

As referred to in Sect. 1 and the system specifications presented in Table 1, namely short-circuit input current and nominal input voltage, a monocrystalline silicon solar PV module, the LG Neon 2 of 350 W [24] was selected. This solar PV module has a 35.3 V voltage at the maximum power point (V_{mpp}) for the standard test conditions. Therefore, was implemented a simulation model using a solar PV physical model on

PSIM, considering the main specifications of the LG Neon 2. Once the parameters of a solar PV module were completed, a string with 34 modules in series was configured, thus constituting the high voltage solar PV panel with a total voltage on the MPP of 1200 V and a maximum power of 11900 W.

3.5 Complete Circuit

Figure 6 presents the diagram of the complete circuit. The MPPT algorithm block puts in the output a reference current that subtracted from the current of each arm will produce the error signals, *Error1* and *Error2*. Each error signal is applied to a PI and its output is compared with a triangular modulating waveform, producing a PWM signal that will command the SiC MOSFET. As explained in chapter 2.2, the modulating waveforms are 180° shifted.

The circuit was simulated for solar radiation intensity variations over time, as presented in Fig. 7. It is possible to observe, that the power at the output of the module, p_{in}, accompanies the maximum power, p_{max}, for the operating conditions. The same is true for the current at the output of the module, i_{in}, which tends to follow the calculated reference current, i_{ref}. The maximum ripple current is within the expected specifications.

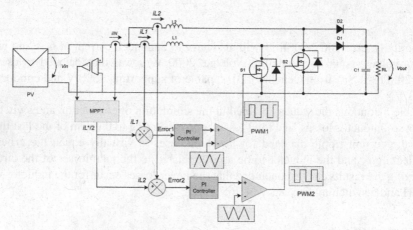

Fig. 6. Schematic diagram of the complete circuit.

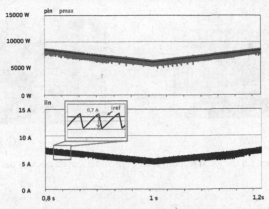

Fig. 7. Simulation of the circuit for variant operating conditions over time with detail of the input current ripple. Module output power, p_{in}; maximum power for operating conditions, p_{max}; output module current, i_{in}; reference current, i_{ref}.

In this section, the experimental results obtained from the system are exposed and analyzed. Results are analyzed in a fragmented way, namely the blocks necessary for the operation of the system, such as converter, PI and MPPT algorithms, and integration with the PV solar module.

4   Experimental Validation

This section describes the development and experimental validation processes of the two-arm IBC prototype. Prototype specifications, presented in Table 5, have been adapted to 1:30 scale reduction compared to the general specifications presented in Table 1.

Adopting a maximum input ripple current (ΔIin) of 10%, based on Eq. (2), the minimum value for the switching frequency is 3.3 kHz. This is a relatively low value, so was chosen a frequency of 20 kHz, resulting in a ripple of 1.7%. The printed circuit board (PCB) developed using Altium software is shown in Fig. 8.

Table 5. Prototype specifications.

Rated input voltage (V_{N_in})	40 V
Open circuit input voltage (V_{OC_in})	50 V
Input current (I_{in})	5 A
Output voltage on the DC bus (V_{out})	66 V
Inductor (L)	6 mH
Capacitor (C)	20 μF

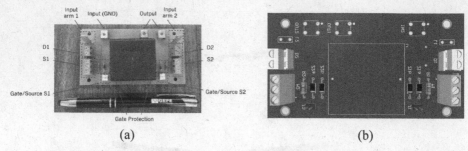

Fig. 8. PCB developed for the DC-DC converter of the interleaved boost type: (a) PCB; (b) Altium 3D model.

The interface circuit between the gate driver output and the power semiconductor gate, as well as the gate protection circuit is composed by a gate-source 10 kΩ resistor, and a 16 V zener diode. The zener diode will protect the SiC in case there are gate voltages higher than allowed by the semiconductor. In turn, the resistor must avoid unwanted transitions in the event of PWM signal failure, imposing the SiC always on cut. It is important to note that the gate resistor is already on the driver circuit side, with a value of 12 Ω, so it has not been placed on the developed PCB.

Figure 9 illustrates the control and power systems integration. The developed PCB and all the components present were attached to a wooden base to facilitate its fixation, organization, and transport. It should be mentioned that each signal conditioning box has four inputs for sensors: two current sensors and two voltage sensors. For this reason, a second signal conditioning box was used to be able to measure i_{in}.

4.1 Power Converter Tests

Preliminary tests to validate the developed hardware were carried out, proving the correct functioning of the open loop system. After, it was validated, initially with a PI control algorithm, to prove its correct operation, imposing a similar current on each arm and them the system was validated with the MPPT control algorithm activated, initially in a controlled laboratory environment and, later, connected to a solar PV module. The results obtained are analyzed in the following topics.

4.1.1 PI Algorithm Tests

To validate the PI algorithm and establish the proportional and integral gains, the test was divided into two stages. In the first one, a 2.25 A reference current was established. Analyzing Fig. 10 (a), it is possible to conclude that I_{in} presents an average value of 2.2 A, obtaining an average value of 1.07 A on i_{L1} and 1.08 A on i_{L2}. Concerning Fig. 10 (b), it is possible to observe the ripple current in each arm for these operating conditions. The correct functioning of the system can be concluded by obtaining a current close to the reference as well as a similar current in each arm.

In the second stage, the reference was varied between 1.5 A and 3.75 A in an interval of 5 s with the same operating conditions. Analysing Fig. 11 (a) it is possible to see that

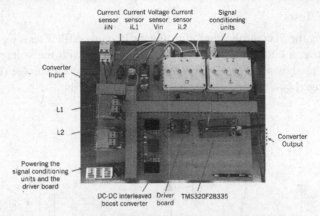

Fig. 9. Integrated system of DC-DC interleaved boost converter.

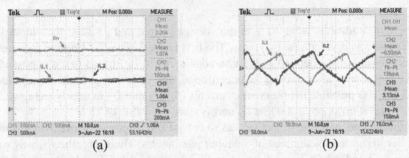

Fig. 10. Experimental results of the PI algorithm with a reference current of 2.25 A: (a) Average value of the currents in each arm, i_{L1} and i_{L2}, and at the input, i_{in}; (b) Ripple of the current on each arm, i_{L1} and i_{L2}.

the system follows the reference current. Regarding Fig. 11 (b) and Fig. 11 (c), it can be concluded that the establishment time is approximately 50 ms.

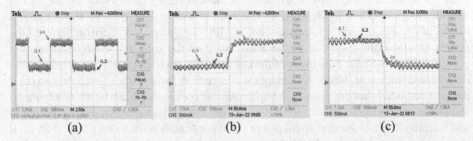

Fig. 11. Experimental results of the PI algorithm with a reference current varying between 1.5 A and 3.75 A: (a) Currents on each arm, i_{L1} and i_{L2}, and at input, i_{in}; (b) Currents on each arm, i_{L1} and i_{L2}, and at the input, i_{in}, in response to the upward current step; (c) Currents on each arm, i_{L1} and i_{L2}, and at the input, i_{in}, in response to the upward rung of current.

4.1.2 MPPT Tests

After validating the PI controller and adjusting the PI gains, MPPT tests were performed. For this purpose, a circuit with a rheostat (R_{in}) in series with the voltage source was implemented, as shown in Fig. 12. Therefore, when the rheostat voltage (v_r) is equal to the input voltage (v_{in}), the maximum power is extracted [25].

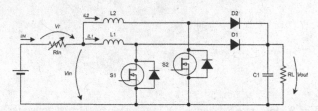

Fig. 12. Scheme used to test MPPT.

The test conditions were 30 V at the voltage source and 28 Ω at the output load, R_L. The test was divided into two parts. The first part consisted of keeping R_{in} equal to 11 Ω and evaluating whether v_{in} and v_r tended to 15 V. In Fig. 13 (a), it is possible to observe that shortly after starting the operation v_{in} and v_r converge to the same value. In Fig. 13 (b), it is possible to observe the currents i_{IN}, i_{L1} and i_{L2} in steady state, whereas in Fig. 13 (c) it turns out again that v_{in} and v_r have the value of 15 V.

In the second part, the objective was to record the response of the MPPT and the controller to sudden oscillations of the input parameters. Therefore, the R_{in} was varied between 8 Ω and 12 Ω. It can be seen in Fig. 14 that at the time instant demarcated with a red line that I_{in} decreased, but v_{in} and v_r remain approximately at the same value, demonstrating a correct functioning of the MPPT algorithm.

4.2 PV Solar Module Tests

The experimental validation was carried out by connecting the power converter to a solar PV module from BP Solar available in the laboratory [26]. From the BP 2150S module, it is important to highlight a maximum power of 150 W, a 34 V voltage at a maximum power of, and a 4.45 A current at MPP. To make a comparison between the results obtained and the point of the actual MPP of the solar PV module, a test was performed in which the duty cycle of the controlled semiconductors was varied and the current and voltage at the converter input was recorded. Analyzing Fig. 15 (a) and (b) it can be concluded that the maximum power point is close to 28 V and 2.85 A. Figure 16 shows the results obtained with the BP 2150S module at 1:26 pm. Analyzing the figure and keeping in mind the maximum power point previously withdrawn (28 V, 2.85 A) it is possible to conclude that the MPPT was successful since the values are very similar.

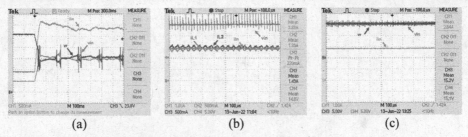

(a) (b) (c)

Fig. 13. Experimental results of the MPPT with $R_{in} = 11\ \Omega$: (a) Voltage in resistance (v_r), Input voltage (v_{in}) and Input current (i_{in}) at the instant the MPPT is connected; (b) Input voltage (v_{in}), currents on each arm and at permanent entry; (c) Voltage in resistance (v_r), Input voltage (v_{in}) and Input current (i_{in}) in the permanent regime.

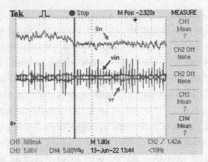

Fig. 14. Experimental results of MPPT when *varying* R_{in}: Voltage in resistance (v_r), Input voltage (v_{in}) and Input current (i_{in}).

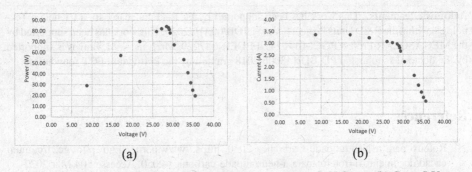

(a) (b)

Fig. 15. Results obtained when varying the duty cycle: (a) P-U Curve; (b) Curve I-V.

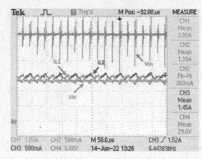

Fig. 16. Results obtained with the BP 2150S module at the 1:26 pm.

5 Conclusions

This paper aims to contribute to the analysis, design and development of a DC-DC power converter for high power solar photovoltaic (PV) applications. A two-arm interleaved topology was chosen, presenting the entire procedure performed for the design of the system. Regarding the control algorithms, the incremental conductance for the Maximum Power Point Tracking (MPPT) control algorithm was used in order to always extract the maximum power from the solar PV system. In turn, in order to impose a balanced current on each arm of the DC-DC power converter, a proportional-integral (PI) control algorithm was implemented. Simulation and experimental results prove the correct functioning of the system. It is concluded that this paper will contribute as a step-by-step guide for engineering students and engineers who intend to develop power electronics solutions for solar PV systems.

Acknowledgements. This work has been supported by FCT – Fundação para a Ciência e Tecnologia within the R&D Units Project Scope: UIDB/00319/2020. This work has been supported by the MEGASOLAR Project POCI-01–0247-FEDER-047220. Mr. Luis A. M. Barros is supported by the doctoral scholarship PD/BD/143006/2018 granted by the Portuguese FCT foundation.

References

1. Roteiro para a Neutralidade Carbónica 2050. https://www.portugal.gov.pt/pt/gc21/comuni cacao/documento?i=roteiro-para-a-neutralidade-carbonica-2050. Accessed 04 Mar 2022
2. Acabou: Central do Pego produziu energia a carvão pela última vez https://www.jn.pt/local/ noticias/santarem/abrantes/acabou-central-do-pego-produziu-energia-a-carvao-pela-ultima-vez-14338710.html. Accessed 23 Sep 2022
3. Rodrigues, J.V.: Portugal pode ter 80% da energia de fontes renováveis já em 2025 https://www.dinheirovivo.pt/empresas/portugal-pode-ter-80-da-energia-de-fontes-ren ovaveis-ja-em-2025-14604140.html. Accessed 04 Mar 2022
4. De Soto, W., Klein, S.A., Beckman, W.A.: Improvement and validation of a model for photovoltaic array performance. Sol. Energy **80**(1), 78–88 (2006)
5. de Barros, L.A.M.: Desenvolvimento de um microinversor com armazenamento local de energia para aplicações solares fotovoltaicas, Universidade do Minho. (2016)

6. da Costa Padilha, F.J.: Topologias de Conversores CC-CC Não Isolados com Saidas Simétricas para Sistemas Fotovoltáicos, Programa de Pós-graduaçã em Engenharia Elétrica, COPPE, Universidade Federal do Rio de Janeiro. (2011)
7. Sousa, T.J., Monteiro, V., Nova, B., Passos, F., Cunha, J., Afonso, J. L.: Parallel Association of Power Semiconductors: an Experimental Evaluation with IGBTs and MOSFETs, In: 2019 International Young Engineers Forum (YEF-ECE), pp. 8–13 (2019)
8. Beheshti, M.: Wide-bandgap semiconductors: performance and benefits of GaN versus SiC, ADJ 4Q. Texas Instruments (2020)
9. Forouzesh, M., Siwakoti, Y.P., Gorji, S.A., Blaabjerg, F., Lehman, B.: Step-up DC-DC converters: a comprehensive review of voltage-boosting techniques, topologies, and applications. IEEE Trans. Power Electron. **32**(12), 9143–9178 (2017)
10. Bhunia, M., Gupta, R., Subudhi, B.: Cascaded DC-DC converter for a reliable standalone PV fed DC load, In: 2014 IEEE 6th India International Conference on Power Electronics (IICPE), pp. 1–6 (2014)
11. Hu, Y., Ioinovici, A.: Simple switched-capacitor-boost converter with large DC gain and low voltage stress on switches. In: IEEE International Symposium on Circuits and Systems (ISCAS) **2015**, 2101–2104 (2015)
12. Abdel-Rahim, O., Orabi, M., Abdelkarim, E., Ahmed, M., Youssef, M.Z.: Switched inductor boost converter for PV applications,. In: 27th **2012**, 2100–2106 (2012)
13. Buerger, R. Péres, Hausmann, R., Reiter, R., Stankiewicz, A.: Ripple analyze and design considerations for an interleaved boost converter (IBC) for a PV source, In: International Conference, ICREPQ (2014)
14. Jang, Y., Jovanovic, M.M.: Interleaved Boost Converter With Intrinsic Voltage-Doubler Characteristic for Universal-Line PFC Front End. Power Electron. IEEE Trans **22**(4), 1394–1401 (2007)
15. Sirdi, N.K.M., Rabhi, A., Nehme, B.: Review of the Best MPPT Algorithms for Control of PV Sources-RUCA Tracking Algorithm., in ICINCO (1), pp. 318–325 (2017)
16. Mustafi'c, D. Joki'c, D., Lale, S., Lubura, S.: Implementation of Incremental Conductance MPPT Algorithm in Real Time in Matlab/Simulink Environment with Humusoft MF634 Board, In: 2020 9th Mediterranean Conference on Embedded Computing (MECO), pp. 1–5 (2020)
17. Barros, L.A., Tanta, M., Sousa, T.J., Afonso, J.L., Pinto, J.: New multifunctional isolated microinverter with integrated energy storage system for PV applications. Energies **13**(15), 4016 (2020)
18. Gkoutioudi, E., Bakas, P., Marinopoulos, A.: Comparison of PV systems with maximum DC voltage 1000V and 1500V, In: 2013 IEEE 39th Photovoltaic Specialists Conference (PVSC), pp. 2873–2878 (2013)
19. Choi, U.-M., Ryu, T.: Comparative evaluation of efficiency and reliability of single-phase five-level NPC inverters for photovoltaic systems. IEEE Access **9**, 120638–120651 (2021)
20. He, J., Sangwongwanich, A., Yang, Y., Iannuzzo, F.: Enhanced reliability of 1500-v photovoltaic inverters with junction temperature limit control, In: 2021 IEEE 12th Energy Conversion Congress & Exposition-Asia (ECCE-Asia), pp. 243–249 (2021)
21. PowerSim, Tutorial: Loss Calculation and Transient Analysis of SiC and GaN Devices. PSIM, (2018)
22. Mfg., H.: High frequency reactors (197 series) https://www.hammfg.com/electronics/transf ormers/choke/197
23. GeneSiC, Datasheet: G2R120MT33J 3300 V 120 ohm SiC MOSFET (2021)
24. LG, Datasheet: LG Neon 2 350W I 345W. (2019)
25. Slinger, S., Efrati, S., Alon, M., Shmilovitz, D.. Maximum Electrical Power Extraction from Sources by Load Matching. Energies **14**(23), 8025 (2021)
26. BP Solar, Datasheet: BP 2150S (2001)

Author Index

J. L. Afonso et al. (Eds.): SESC 2022, LNICST 502, p. 127, 2023.
https://doi.org/10.1007/978-3-031-33979-0

Printed in the United States
by Baker & Taylor Publisher Services